Salecology®

Dominate in a Downturn

Darren Bezani

Salecology®
Dominate in a Downturn
Darren Bezani

ISBN 978-1-917109-36-9

A CIP catalogue record for this book is available from the British Library.

Published 2024
Tricorn Books,
Treadgolds
Bishop Street
Portsmouth PO1 3HN
www.tricornbooks.co.uk

Salecology®

Dominate in a Downturn

Contents

forces 5

About the Author

Darren Bezani is a master of sales strategy and a transformative leader whose guidance has rocketed organisations from Series B infancy to multi-billion-dollar valuations. At the helm of Salecology, he's renowned for his visionary approach to sales excellence and leadership acumen, having championed change and spurred growth across the globe. His methodologies have permeated the commercial landscapes across the Americas, EMEA, and Asia Pacific, and his innovative methods adopted in over 85 countries and translated into 16 different languages.

Bezani's stellar reputation is built on a foundation of real-world successes, where his strategic interventions have recalibrated the trajectory of start-ups, scale-ups, and global titans alike. Bezani's newest publication introduces the 'Five Force Model', a cutting-edge blueprint for building sales organisations that not only meet but surpass their ambitious targets. Here the five force model is utilised in tough economic conditions, but they are equally powerful in more buoyant times. It's a compendium of breakthrough tactics that have empowered organisations to ascend to peak performance and shatter sales records.

In this book, Bezani reveals the core principles that propel the elite, and learn how to forge a high-calibre sales organisation that rewrites the rules of success. Readers are invited to experience the evolution of business through Bezani's proven strategies for achieving sustainable, high-impact growth.

Introduction

Since World War 2, we have seen an economic recession take place on average every 5 years and they last approximately 18 months. An interesting statistic, predominately given to us from the financing industry as they look at when the Bear markets start and stop, and when we enter a period of expansion. From a sales and business perspective, I am not sure we see it as clearly as the stock market, but we do find times when it is harder to make sales.

We have seen some tough trading periods almost every decade since 1980 and I have seen my fair share; having sold through the one in the late 80s, then the dotcom boom and bust, I have driven growth through the financial crisis that started in 2007, and then helped many clients pivot and win during the pandemic. So I thought it would be a good time to create this book which captures my learnings on how to win in a slow economy, taking lessons from the past, but also sharing what companies are doing right now to continue to grow and dominate in a downturn.

The reality of a recession is that it just gets tougher. Companies' baton down the hatches, lay off employees, freeze spending, and overall just make doing business hard. That said, when you look at GDP, it usually drops somewhere between 2-5%, so people are still buying, it is just that the ripple effect is felt a long way down the food chain. It is the fear of what might come that drives behaviour, and pessimism creeps into the everyday psyche.

The challenge is that it can catch salespeople off guard as they try to keep doing the same approach as when they were in an expansion market. In an expansion market, companies are more optimistic, willing to try new things and open to suggestions, hence easier to gain their attention and they are prepared to listen. Purse strings are a little looser and therefore getting signoff becomes a little easier. The salesperson selling in this marketplace can go a long way with energy, enthusiasm, and personality. Bolt on to that a cool-looking product with cool branding, and chances are the "product sells itself". Of course, I am underplaying it a little, the product must be fit for purpose, and do what it promises, but I think you get the idea.

This style and approach in a slow economy just doesn't work and that is why you see salespeople that go from 'Hero to Zero'. Nice to-haves, premium services, and add-ons all take a back seat when customers look to consolidate their spending. Orders get cancelled, deals become stuck in the pipeline, meetings get postponed, and the salesperson starts to panic. With plummeting sales, not making targets, and eroding commission payments, the salesperson starts to make some adjustments but also a host of mistakes. You often see 2 different strategies come about,

1. Chasing big deals, or
2. Chasing from one small deal to another.

They can move into the role of 'I just need to sell something' and forget about the target customer groups or Ideal Candidate Profile (ICP), market trends and forget about product differentiation, only to settle for selling on Features and Benefits.

To win the deal at any cost will create havoc across the organisation and the customer's organisation. Salespeople will tend to over-promise, and then internal bickering will take place as the delivery team is expected to deliver on the promises.

The sales organisations that thrive during the downturn pivot their approach and must blend a range of aspects in their business, it is not just about becoming more consultative, or more salesy, it's about looking at different elements of it's business that need to align and build the organisation that dominates in a downturn and is poised to go stratospheric as soon as the economy hits the uptick.

Solution Selling is Dead!

The traditional approach of solution selling is increasingly showing its age and let's be honest in a SaaS world it is dead! This doesn't mean that some of the selling techniques don't work, you still need to generate interest, understand customer needs, sell features and benefits, follow up and so on, but it is not enough. Gone are the days when salespeople could play the role of consultants, crafting bespoke solutions for each customer. Today's SaaS landscape demands a different approach, one that acknowledges the reality of selling a pre-packaged service rather than a customizable solution. Salespeople are no longer building solutions from the ground up;

they are guiding customers towards a predefined product that has already proven its worth in the market.

This shift is underpinned by three core aspects:

1: A defined target audience and segment,
2: A predetermined set of hypotheses about customer challenges, and
3: A packaged solution with established metrics.

Salespeople are expected to identify and engage with a specific audience, understand their presumed challenges, and present a ready-made solution that aligns with these understanding and customisation that traditional solution selling promised.

Success also isn't just about having a superior product or service. It's about understanding the intricate dance of market dynamics, customer expectations, and innovative strategies. To thrive, especially in challenging economic conditions, businesses need a holistic approach that addresses the multifaceted challenges they face.

Herein lies the need for a paradigm shift, a move away from the old-school thinking of solution selling to embracing the five forces imperative for SaaS success: Disruptive Mindset, Insight Agility, Client Centricity, Distinctive Dominance, and Emotional Intelligence. These forces represent a holistic approach to SaaS sales, one that transcends the limitations of solution selling.

Disruptive Mindset challenges the status quo, encouraging innovative thinking and adaptability in a fast-paced market. Insight Agility emphasises the importance of quickly turning market data into actionable strategies, moving beyond the static approach of traditional solution selling. Client Centricity puts the focus on deeply understanding and exceeding customer expectations, ensuring that the pre-packaged solutions are effectively meeting the evolving needs of the market. Distinctive Dominance is about carving out a unique space in the crowded SaaS market, something that solution selling, with its one-size-fits-all approach, often fails to achieve. Finally, Emotional Intelligence ensures that all interactions, both internal and external, are handled with empathy and effective communication, crucial for building lasting relationships in the SaaS industry.

The Five Force Model

In today's SaaS world, clinging to the methodologies of solution selling is akin to bringing a knife to a gunfight. It's not just about selling a product; it's about understanding the market, the customer, and the unique value proposition of your offering. The five forces provide a comprehensive framework for this understanding, ensuring that SaaS companies can thrive in an ever-evolving landscape.

1. **Disruptive Mindset:** Embrace a disruptor's mindset, challenge the status quo, and continuously evolve to stay ahead of emerging trends and needs.
2. **Insightful Agility:** Stay ahead of market shifts with data-driven insights, a nimble approach to strategy & execution, and packaging insight for the hands of sales and marketing.
3. **Client Centricity:** Deepen client relationships by understanding their unique challenges and delivering undeniable value at every interaction, with a focus on growing and expanding customer accounts.
4. **Distinctive Dominance:** Understand and secure your competitive edge, show you customers the blueprint for success and secure brand loyalty with strong feedback loops and advocacy incentive programmes.
5. **Emotional Intelligence:** Truly understand and connect with clients, enhance team dynamics and collaboration, navigate sales with emotion, and build a resilient business with emotional foresight.

The ability to not just survive but thrive in both challenging economic climates and fluctuating market conditions is paramount. This resilience and adaptability are rooted in a deep understanding and strategic application of each of the five critical forces: These forces are not just individual pillars of strength; they are interconnected elements that, when combined, form a robust framework for enduring success.

The Disruptive Mindset is the catalyst for innovation and adaptability, enabling SaaS companies to anticipate and respond to market shifts with agility and creativity. Insight Agility empowers these companies to harness data and analytics effectively, turning insights into actionable strategies that keep them ahead of the curve. Client Centricity ensures that the evolving needs and expectations of customers are not just met but exceeded, fostering loyalty and long-term relationships. Distinctive Dominance is about carving out a unique competitive advantage, setting a SaaS company apart in a crowded marketplace. Lastly, Emotional Intelligence is the glue that binds all these forces together, ensuring that internal and external interactions are handled with empathy, understanding, and effective communication.

Disruptive Mindset

In the rapidly evolving SaaS industry, a disruptive mindset is not just beneficial, it's essential. This force is about embracing change, challenging conventional wisdom, and constantly seeking innovative solutions. It's a mindset that doesn't just adapt to change – it anticipates and drives it. Companies that cultivate a disruptive mindset in their people are always a step ahead, identifying and capitalizing on new opportunities before their competitors even recognize them. This proactive approach is crucial in a landscape where staying still equates to falling behind.

Insight Agility

Insight Agility is the ability to swiftly gather, analyse, and act upon market and customer data. In the digital age, data is abundant, but the real competitive advantage lies in how quickly and effectively a company can convert this data into actionable insights. This force is about being agile enough to respond to real-time information, adapting strategies on the fly, and making informed decisions that keep the company aligned with market demands and ahead of competitors.

Client Centricity

Client Centricity places the customer at the heart of every business decision. It's about understanding that the success of a SaaS company is inextricably linked to the success of its clients. This force emphasizes building deep, empathetic relationships with customers, truly understanding their needs and challenges, and consistently delivering value that goes beyond the technology itself. Client Centricity is not just about customer satisfaction, it's about customer success, loyalty, and advocacy.

Distinctive Dominance

Distinctive Dominance is about carving out a unique position in the market and maintaining a competitive edge. It's the ability to not just compete but to set the standards in your industry. This force involves a deep understanding of your unique value proposition, clear differentiation from competitors, and a relentless focus on innovation. Companies that achieve distinctive dominance are seen as leaders and trendsetters, commanding respect and loyalty from both customers and competitors.

Emotional Intelligence

Emotional Intelligence is the often-overlooked force that can make or break relationships in the business world. It encompasses self-awareness, empathy, and the ability to manage one's own emotions and understand others'. For the individual, self regulation, resilience in a tough market and embracing a growth mindset will keep them motivated to win. In the context of SaaS and Tech sales, emotional intelligence is critical for building strong relationships with clients, navigating complex negotiations, and fostering a collaborative and productive work environment. It's about connecting with people on a human level, which is essential in a sector where technology often takes centre stage.

The Synergy of the Five Forces for SaaS Success

In the intricate tapestry of the tech landscape, especially during economic downturns, the threads of strategy, innovation, and understanding are interwoven, creating a resilient fabric that can weather any storm. The Five Forces, while powerful on their own, derive their true strength from their collective synergy.

The dance between **Disruptive Mindset** and **Client Centricity** is a testament to this. As businesses continuously innovate and challenge the status quo, they craft solutions that resonate deeply with clients' evolving needs. This constant evolution ensures that offerings remain not just relevant but indispensable, deepening the bond between the business and its clientele.

Yet, understanding clients is just one piece of the puzzle. This profound knowledge paves the way for **Distinctive Dominance**. Recognizing what truly sets a business apart in the crowded market allows it to carve a niche for itself. This unique positioning, rooted in client insights, ensures that businesses remain the preferred choice, standing tall amidst competitors.

However, the SaaS world is ever-changing. Dominance today does not guarantee dominance tomorrow. This is where **Insightful Agility** comes into play. With a clear competitive advantage as the foundation, businesses must remain nimble, adapting swiftly to market shifts. By making data-driven decisions and anticipating trends, they ensure that their dominance isn't fleeting but sustained.

Yet, in this data-driven world, the human element remains paramount. **Emotional Intelligence** bridges the gap between cold hard facts and the warm nuances of human interactions. While agility ensures businesses stay ahead of market trends, emotional intelligence ensures they stay attuned to the emotional undercurrents of their clients. This blend of insights and empathy allows businesses to make decisions that resonate on both practical and emotional levels.

Interestingly, it's this emotional connection that circles back to innovation. Truly understanding clients, feeling their challenges, and empathizing with their aspirations provides fertile ground for **Disruptive Mindset**. By addressing both the tangible and intangible needs of clients, businesses can craft solutions that not only solve problems but also evoke trust, loyalty, and satisfaction.

In essence, each of the Five Forces are not isolated strategies but interconnected facets of a holistic approach. Each force, while formidable on its own, draws strength from the others, creating a robust and resilient strategy that ensures businesses don't just survive but thrive, even in the most challenging economic conditions.

How to use this book

In a landscape where change is the only constant, these five forces provide a comprehensive approach to not just weathering storms but also capitalizing on opportunities. They ensure that SaaS and tech companies remain flexible, responsive, and ahead of the game, regardless of the economic climate or market changes. This book delves into each of these forces, offering insights, strategies, and real-world examples to help companies harness their full potential and chart a course for sustained success.

You will see each force has its own section of the book enabling you to dip into each element and understand its impact as well as how to implement elements in your business to bring it to life. At the back of the book you will find how to synergise the different forces, whether you focus on two, three, four or all five forces into action.

Force 1: Disruptive Mindset

1

Dm

1

Dm

Contents

Disruptive Mindset

Within the SaaS world innovation is the lifeblood that ensures survival, growth, and dominance. But what does it truly mean to be Disruptive and have a "Disruptive Mindset"? It goes beyond merely introducing new features or tweaking user interfaces. It's about cultivating a mindset, a culture, and a relentless drive to challenge the status quo, to see beyond the present, and to shape the future.

In a world that's constantly evolving, resting on one's laurels is a recipe for obsolescence. The disruptor's mindset is characterized by an insatiable curiosity, a willingness to question established norms, and the audacity to envision and create something ground-breaking. It's not about change for the sake of change but about meaningful evolution that addresses unmet needs, taps into emerging trends, and offers unparalleled value.

Every industry giant, every market leader, was once a challenger—a disruptor that dared to do things differently. In the realm of technology, where competition can be fierce and barriers to entry are often low, or at least barriers to replicating features and benefits are low, challenging the status quo is not just an option, it's a necessity. This means continuously analysing current practices, offerings, and strategies, seeking out inefficiencies, gaps, or areas of potential enhancement, and having the courage to make the changes needed. One needs to challenge the Status Quo of their own business and approaches, but also learn how to challenge the customers thinking, especially when the economic outlook changes.

Therefore, innovation isn't a one-time event - it's a continuous journey. Technology, with its rapid advancements and shifting user expectations, demands businesses to be in a state of perpetual evolution. This means staying abreast of industry trends, technological advancements, and competitor moves. It involves fostering a culture where feedback, both from clients and internal teams, is valued and acted upon. And most importantly, it requires a commitment to invest in research, development, and training to ensure the business remains at the cutting edge.

Behind every innovative breakthrough lies a vision—a clear, compelling picture of what could be. This vision acts as a north star, guiding strategies, inspiring teams, and attracting clients. For SaaS businesses, having a clear vision means understanding where the industry is headed, anticipating future challenges and opportunities, and crafting a roadmap to navigate this future landscape successfully. But what about those who are at the customer facing end? Each individual sales person needs to have their own vision. I am talking about their own personal, deeply held beliefs about how to reshape the market, challenge the norms and introduce transformative solutions. It is their vision that provides a unique perspective on how the product or service can redefine the market, solve pressing challenges and usher in new possibilities. It is their vision, combined with the organisation, that differentiates them and the service from everyone else.

In this section of the book, we'll delve deeper into 4 core areas:

The Disruptive Mindset:	the catalyst for change and building it into the organisation
Challenging the Status Quo:	how to reframe the customer's mind with insight-led conversations
Building Continuous Evolution:	how to craft a strategy to stay ahead of trends and changes
The Power of Vision:	how to craft a vision for both the organisation and how to help the sales team create their vision.

Each of these facets, offering insights, strategies, and actionable steps to truly harness the power of Innovative Impact. From cultivating the right mindset to implementing tangible strategies, we'll explore how SaaS and tech businesses can position themselves at the forefront of innovation, ensuring unparalleled success in a dynamic market.

The Disruptive Mindset is the Catalyst

Interestingly, we have seen over the last couple of decades that it is those companies that come in with a product that disrupt the market, they have an impact on the market, make people listen and have rapid growth. In the ever-evolving world of tech there's a truth you must confront: if you're not moving forward, you're falling behind. Economic downturns, while challenging, present a unique canvas for those daring enough to paint a different picture. At the heart of this audacious approach is the disruptive mindset. It's not just about tweaking what's been done before, it's about re-imagining the entire game. And in a slow economy, this mindset isn't just beneficial—it's essential.

The disruptive mindset needs to be embedded across the whole organisation, it is not just about the visionary leader. It needs to be in the product team, design team, leadership team, and definitely within the sales team. After all, it is this disruptive mindset that will lead the customer to understand 'Why they should change' from what they are currently doing or switch from the products and solutions they already have.

The Imperative of Disruption

Think of a disruptive mindset as your secret weapon. It's not about making incremental changes or slight improvements. No, it's about revolutionizing how you approach challenges, seeing them not as barriers but as opportunities to redefine your market. When the economic going gets tough, many businesses hunker down, playing it safe. But you? With a disruptive mindset, you see a playground ripe for innovation, and set your team on a course of driving change.

In a sluggish economy, the rules of the game change. Market dynamics can shift overnight. While many might see this as a threat, you should recognize it as an opportunity. By anticipating these shifts, you position yourself ahead of the curve, ready to seize new opportunities while others are still scrambling to understand the changes.

Moreover, when businesses face challenges, there's a tendency to converge, to adopt similar, 'safe' strategies. This leads to a saturated, indistinguishable market. But with a disruptive mindset, you stand out. You offer something unique, something competitors haven't even thought of, let alone offered.

And here's the kicker: while many see a slow economy as a time to tighten the belt and brace for impact, you see a launchpad. By addressing emerging needs with innovative solutions, you don't just survive—you thrive and grow.

Cultivating Your Disruptive Mindset

Alright – enough of why! How do you get it, and more importantly, how do we build it into the organisation? First and foremost, foster a culture of curiosity within your organization. Encourage your teams to challenge the status quo. Create an environment where questions are celebrated, where the phrases "Why?" and "What if?" echo in every meeting.

But it's not enough to just ask questions. You must also be willing to take some risks. In many organizations, there's a fear of failure, especially when the market has turned. Celebrate the risks, the attempts and the daring ventures into the unknown. Because it's there, in the uncharted territories, that true disruption is born. This is easier said than done, especially when the pressure is on to continue to perform and grow.

The answer is to equip yourself and your teams with the tools to think big. This might mean attending workshops on the latest technologies, engaging with industry pioneers, or setting aside time for brainstorming sessions. The key is to always be learning and always be growing. And don't just look inward. The world outside is teeming with ideas, with innovations waiting to be discovered. Engage with other industries, collaborate with startups, and attend conferences. Bring in fresh perspectives, and let them mingle with your own.

Remember that disruption is a continuous journey. Prototype, get feedback, iterate, and if necessary, pivot. Move swiftly, adapt, and keep your eyes on the horizon.

Inspire: Stories of Disruption and success

While innovation is the engine that drives disruption, inspiration is the fuel. Sharing compelling success stories serves a dual purpose: it showcases the tangible benefits of your product and motivates potential clients to envision similar success for themselves.

Success stories

Build Trust: When potential clients hear about others who've achieved significant growth or outpaced competitors using your solution, it builds trust. It's evidence that your product delivers on its promises.

Humanise Your Product: Success stories put a human face to your product. They transform it from a mere tool to a catalyst for growth, success, and transformation.

Crafting Compelling Success Stories

Success stories are more than just endorsements, they're narratives that showcase the transformative power of your product. When crafted effectively, they resonate deeply, influencing potential clients and reinforcing the trust of existing ones.

Gathering Real Testimonials

The authenticity of a success story lies in its genuineness. Instead of relying on generic endorsements, it's crucial to reach out to satisfied clients and invite them to share their experiences. These first-hand accounts, brimming with genuine emotions and challenges overcome, strike a chord with potential clients. They see themselves in these stories, making the journey from scepticism to trust, from curiosity to conviction. By showcasing real people with real challenges who've achieved real success with your solution, you're offering potential clients a glimpse into their potential journey

Highlighting Tangible Benefits:

While the emotional resonance of a success story is undeniably powerful, it's the tangible benefits that often seal the deal. It's essential to emphasize the concrete outcomes achieved by clients using your product. Did they witness a surge in their revenue? Were they able to save significant amounts of time, leading to increased efficiency? Or perhaps they managed to carve a niche and expand their market share? By spotlighting these tangible achievements, you're not just telling potential clients that success is possible; you're showing them. It provides a clear picture of the measurable benefits they can expect, making the decision to onboard with your solution that much easier.

Using Various Mediums to Share Stories

The medium is as crucial as the message. In today's digital age, potential clients consume content in myriad ways. While written testimonials have their place, diversifying the mediums can amplify the reach and impact of success stories. Consider video interviews, where clients can visually and vocally express their journey, making the experience more relatable. Podcasts offer an auditory experience, allowing potential clients to listen on the go. Infographics, with their blend of visuals and data, can succinctly convey the before-and-after transformation achieved with your product. By leveraging various mediums, you ensure that your success stories reach a broader audience, each segment consuming it in a way that resonates most with them.

In weaving these success stories, remember that you're not just showcasing the efficacy of your product; you're spotlighting the human element, the transformative journeys of individuals and businesses. These narratives, authentic and impactful, serve as beacons, guiding potential clients towards making a decision that could redefine their own success trajectories.

While a disruptive mindset lays the foundation for success, it's the continuous cycle of innovation and the power of inspiration that propel businesses forward. By emphasizing the importance of evolution and sharing compelling success stories, you not only solidify your position in the market but inspire others to embark on their journeys of disruption and growth.

Challenging the Status Quo

In business, the status quo is a double-edged sword. On one side, it offers the comfort of familiarity, a tried-and-tested path that promises consistent, albeit stagnant, results. On the flip side, it's a barrier, a cognitive chain that restricts innovation and growth. To truly thrive, especially in a slow economy, challenging the status quo isn't just recommended, it's imperative. As we get stuck into the concept let's understand some of the psychological aspects first.

Understanding the Status Quo Bias

At its core, the status quo Bias is a cognitive bias that favours the current situation. It's a psychological preference for the familiar, a resistance to change. This bias stems from our innate desire for consistency and predictability. Change, even if potentially beneficial, is often perceived as a threat, introducing uncertainty and potential risks.

But why do we cling to the familiar, even when evidence suggests there might be a better way? The answer lies in another cognitive bias: loss aversion. We're wired to feel the pain of a loss more acutely than the pleasure of a gain. So, the potential risks associated with change, even if they're minor, often overshadow the potential benefits in our minds.

Loss Aversion – it's a lot more than FOMO.

Amid an economic downturn, it's natural for people to feel a heightened sense of caution. The world around them seems to be contracting, businesses are shuttering, and the future appears uncertain. This environment fosters a psychological phenomenon known as loss aversion. But what if, instead of succumbing to this fear, you chose to challenge the status quo and turn adversity into opportunity?

In 1979, psychologists Daniel Kahneman and Amos Tversky, published an academic paper which discussed 'loss aversion' as part of their research on decision-making under uncertainty. This paper, and subsequent research into cognitive bias, helped Kahneman go on to receive a Nobel Prize in economics. They found that people typically experience about twice as much psychological pain from a loss as they do pleasure from an equivalent gain. For example, losing $100 may be more painful than the pleasure received from winning $100. People are more motivated to avoid losses than they are to pursue gains. In a slow economy, this fear of loss becomes magnified. Every decision, every risk, and every potential investment is viewed through a lens tinted with the fear of potential setbacks.

According to Dan Ariely (Predictably Irrational), there are lots of reasons why loss aversion can stop people from buying.

These include:

- Status quo bias
- Residual satisfaction
- Cost (time and money)
- Fear of making the wrong choice
- FOMO

It is easy to accept that during a challenging economy, people will rather stick with what they have or 'make do' with things as they already are. But here's the thing: while a slow economy does present challenges, it also offers unique opportunities for those willing to look beyond immediate threats and envision long-term potential. The key is to understand your own loss aversion, confront it, and then strategically navigate through it.

Firstly, recognize that loss aversion is a natural human instinct. It's a protective mechanism that has evolved over millennia to keep you safe from potential threats. In the modern economic landscape, this translates to a reluctance to invest in new ventures or take risks that might lead to financial loss. However, by acknowledging this inherent bias, you can start to see it for what it is: a psychological barrier, not an insurmountable reality. To win the customer over, and get them to see the opportunity, you must first be able to challenge the status quo bias that will exist. To be fair, this is true in any situation, not just an economic downturn, but it is just heightened during this time.

The Cost of Not Challenging the Status Quo

Before we explore how to challenge the Status Quo, let us understand that it comes with significant costs:

- **Stagnation:** In a rapidly evolving industry sticking to the familiar can quickly lead to obsolescence.
- **Missed Opportunities:** By not exploring new avenues or solutions, businesses miss out on potential growth opportunities.
- **Reduced Competitive Edge:** As competitors innovate and evolve, clinging to the status quo can erode a business's competitive advantage.

In the last couple of recessions, I have had the opportunity to work with many businesses that utilised the time to continue to drive forward, and interestingly, all of them came out the back end of the recession faster and beat the competition into a pulp.

Frame of Reference

In order to challenge the status quo we need to consider perception and understanding, and in particular the concept of a 'Frame of Reference' plays a pivotal role. It refers to the set of criteria or stated values in relation to which measurements or judgments can be made. More than a mere technical term, it's a lens through which individuals view, process, and interpret the world around them. This frame is shaped by a myriad of factors: cultural background, personal experiences, education, and even the language we speak. These elements collectively form an invisible scaffold that supports and influences our interpretation of events, ideas, and interactions.

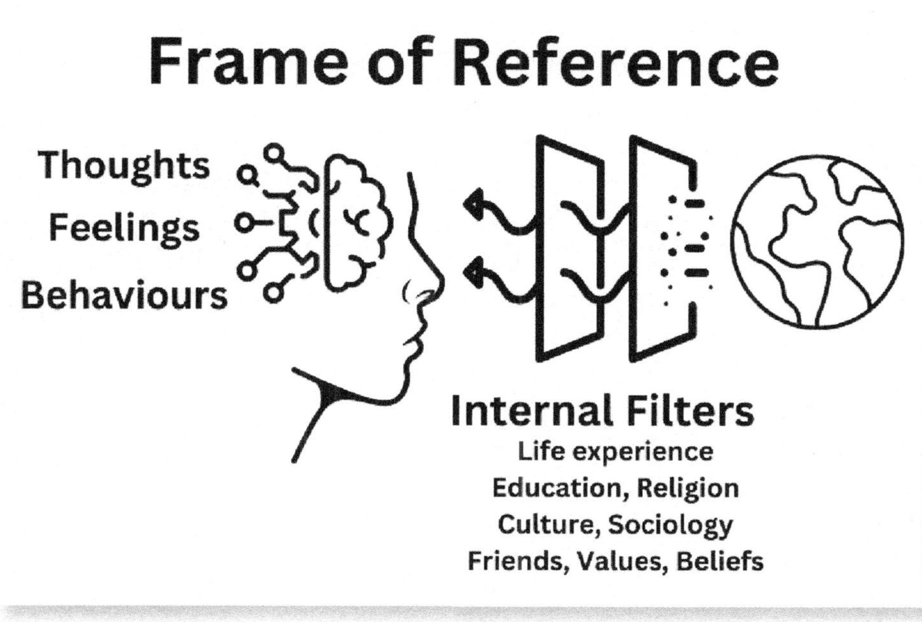

The power of the Frame of Reference is most evident in the diversity of human thought. Two individuals might observe the same event, yet their descriptions might vary drastically, coloured by their unique frames. In his article 'Your Frame of Reference Influences Your Decision Making' published in Personnel Today, Matt Grawitch discusses how a frame of reference is the context within which we interpret the world, evaluate various decision options, and reach conclusions. He breaks down the frame of reference into two key elements: the decision context and the psychological context. The decision context refers to the specifics of the decision situation, while the psychological context refers to the decision maker's interpretations of the situation, influenced by attitudes, beliefs, and prior experiences.

In times of economic recession, the Frame of Reference becomes a crucial tool for understanding and navigating the challenges posed by a contracting economy. For individuals, their frame of reference is often shaped by their personal experiences with financial stability, job security, and previous economic downturns. This influences their spending habits, investment decisions, and their overall outlook on the economy. For instance, someone who experienced significant losses in a previous recession may become more conservative in their financial decisions, prioritizing savings over spending or investments. Conversely, an individual who has not faced such hardships might remain more optimistic and willing to take risks, believing in a quick recovery.

For businesses, the Frame of Reference encompasses the collective mindset of its leadership and organizational culture. During a recession, companies often have to make critical decisions - whether to cut costs, invest in new markets, or pivot their business model. These decisions are heavily influenced by the leadership's past experiences, industry norms, and the perceived state of the economy. A business leader who has successfully navigated past recessions may rely on similar strategies, while another might decide to take a completely different approach based on their interpretation of current market conditions. Moreover, businesses must also consider the frames of reference of their consumers, whose spending patterns are affected by the economic climate. Understanding these perspectives is vital for businesses to adapt their strategies, whether it's in marketing, product development, or customer engagement.

In both personal and business realms, the Frame of Reference during a recession often dictates the balance between risk and caution. It shapes how entities perceive opportunities and threats in a constrained economic environment. This is why it's essential for both individuals and businesses to periodically re-evaluate their frames of reference. By acknowledging biases and limitations in their perspectives, they can make more informed, adaptive, and resilient decisions in the face of economic adversity.

Reframing the Narrative

The fundamental element of getting customers to engage into a sales conversation and look to buy anything is to answer the 'Why Change'. The disruptive mindset will need to reframe the customers' mind and assist them in seeing things differently.

Reframing, as described by cognitive psychologist George Lakoff, is about changing the way the public sees the world. It's about presenting a new frame that fits the facts of a situation and thus leads to a shift in understanding. In sales, this means helping customers see a problem, solution, or decision in a new light.

Reframing is not about changing the facts but altering the lens through which we view them. For instance, a slow economy can be seen as a period of decline, or it can be viewed as a time ripe for innovation and new opportunities. The facts remain the same, but the narrative changes.

Here are some examples of different situations where the customer's frame of reference is holding them back and the use of reframing for them to see things differently.

Case 1: Cloud-Based Storage Solutions
Situation: A company was hesitant to transition from its traditional on-premises storage systems to a cloud-based solution, fearing security breaches and data loss.

Reframing: The salesperson reframed the situation by emphasizing the evolution of cloud security. Instead of focusing on the change, they highlighted how top cloud providers invest millions in security measures, often making cloud storage more secure than traditional systems. They also pointed out the added benefits of accessibility, scalability, and cost savings. By reframing the cloud solution to enhance security and efficiency, the company was more receptive to the transition.

Case 2: CRM Software for Small Businesses

Situation: A small business owner believed that CRM (Customer Relationship Management) software was only for large corporations and would be too complex for their operations.

Reframing: The sales representative introduced a CRM tailored for small businesses. They reframed the software not as a complex system for big corporations but as a tool to understand customers better, streamline sales processes, and grow the business. By emphasizing the scalability and user-friendliness of the software, the small business owner recognized its potential value.

Case 3: Transitioning to a Subscription-Based Model

Situation: A graphic design software company wanted to transition its customers from a one-time purchase model to a subscription-based model. Many long-time users were resistant, seeing the subscription model as more expensive and less valuable.

Reframing: The company highlighted the continuous updates, added features, and constant support that came with the subscription model. They reframed the subscription not as a recurring cost but as a way to always have the latest tools and features at one's fingertips. By emphasizing the ongoing value and innovation, many customers saw the benefits of the new model.

Case 4: Implementing AI Solutions

Situation: A retail business was approached with an AI-driven inventory management solution. The business owner was sceptical, believing AI to be an overhyped buzzword with little practical value.

Reframing: The salesperson demonstrated how AI could predict inventory needs based on historical data, seasonal trends, and market shifts. They reframed the AI solution not as a trendy tech addition but as a way to reduce overstock, minimize stockouts, and optimize inventory levels. By showcasing tangible benefits, the retailer was convinced of the solution's value.

In each of these cases, reframing was used to shift the perspective of potential buyers, helping them see the value and benefits of the software or solution being offered. This approach not only addresses concerns and objections but also highlights the unique advantages that the solution can bring to the table.

For your customers, this reframing can be the difference between holding back and taking the leap to invest in your solution. If they're entrenched with a frame of reference of fear and loss, they're less likely to see the value in what you offer. Your role is to help them shift this narrative and utilise that loss aversion as part of the need to change.

Educating the Customer

Education is a powerful tool in the reframing process. When customers understand the broader context, the potential benefits of a product or service and the long-term implications of the service. The better equipped they are to make informed decisions.

You'll see in a later chapter when we look at insight agility about why it's important to have insight into the market trends, economies and emerging opportunities, and also how to utilise case studies in the education process. However, lets us understand the impact of educating the customer.

In 'The Challenger Sales Rep' book, Dixon and Adamson discuss 'Teaching for Differentiation' and the impact of helping customers understand problems or challenges that they may not realise they have.

Sales enablement teams have spent small fortunes on teaching the sales team how to conduct great discovery calls with questioning techniques and alike. This has been useful if the customer knows what their needs are. Unfortunately, what happens if the customer doesn't know what their needs are? What if their real need is to have someone to tell them what they need! Apple is a great example of this, they don't invent products by asking the world what it needs, they invent products and say, hey look at this, you didn't know you needed it, but you will love this!

The Disruptive mindset needs to be able to challenge the Status Quo and grab the attention of potentially reluctant customers to think differently.

Emotion Drives Motion

In the Salecology book, Unleash Your Sales SuperPower, we shared the dynamic of IQ vs. EQ and looked at Roger W. Sperry's concept of the

Left Brain / Right Brain. In essence, the Right Brain looks at the logical rational aspects of your value propositions, and the left brain will be more interested in the emotive aspects of it. Everywhere you look there are some interesting deals to be had, a myriad of products to save or give you more time, save you money, or make you money, make you a better life, increase your health and so on.

But something inside us acts as a compass, leading us towards or away from certain deals. I don't mean because the offers won't help, it means am I really interested? Is this something I want to invest my time and effort on even though it is financially or physically beneficial?

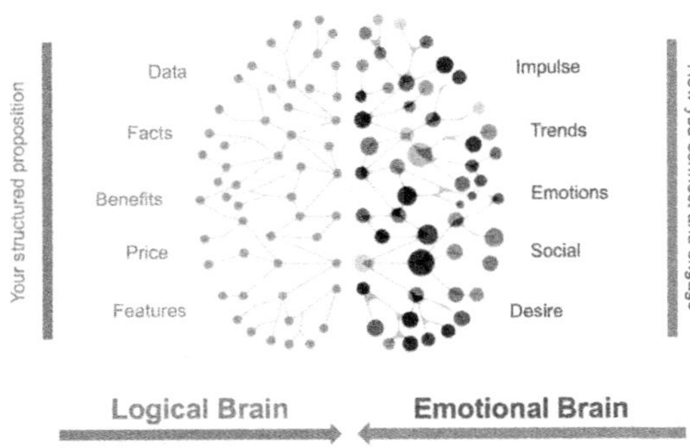

This emotional, irrational part of the brain forms part of our subconscious mind. It is not a conscious thought but more a 'gut feeling'. Harvard Professor Gerald Zaltman identified that up to 95% of all decisions are made in this unconscious part of the mind. Marketeers have been trying to tap into this for generations – product placement on a shelf, colours used on the packaging, and names of products – all designed to conjure up an emotion or affiliation with the product, but salespeople have been somewhat lacking at identifying this key to unlocking an emotional engagement into the deal.

To challenge the status quo, you need to understand that the customer must therefore be emotionally engaged, and a strong compelling value proposition, or ROI (return on investment) won't be enough.

Be someone the customer is willing to pay to spend time with!

A question an old boss used to ask me was: 'would our customers be willing to pay to spend time with our salespeople?' This has stuck with me as it highlighted whether the customer can see value in the time spent with the team. Going through the various attributes of this I have pulled from various research 5 core things which consistently came out as the top priorities for customers to receive from their sales contact:

1.	**Expertise and Insight**:	Customers expect sales reps to be knowledgeable about the industry, products, and market trends.
2.	**Inquisitive Approach**:	Customers want sales reps who understand their unique challenges and offer tailored solutions, rather than generic pitches.
3.	**Authentic Engagement**:	Customers value sales reps who engage with them genuinely, listen actively, and build trust.
4.	**Transparency**:	Honesty, clear communication, and transparency in pricing and product capabilities are crucial.
5.	**Efficient Use of Time**:	In the digital age, customers expect sales reps to respect their time, offer timely responses, and leverage technology for efficient interactions.

Looking at these top 5 reinforces the aspect of where the customer sees value. They see value in people who bring innovative ideas and expertise into their world, challenge assumptions, seek to understand, and don't waste their time. It doesn't say, someone who is good at pitching their products and services, or who can demonstrate their product's features and benefits, or can do a good diagnostic or needs analysis. All of these points interestingly combine the left and right brain. On the surface, these may appear logical and rational aspects, but they provide both. Emotional engagement comes through and connects with the audience as they have a genuine feeling that they are working with someone interested and engaged in the activity, not a 'drive-by' salesperson.

Educate yes, but make sure you lead them to your solution!

One of the common mistakes of sales teams, salespeople, influencers et al, is that they provide education which in essence provides free consulting or training. You have no doubt seen social media videos, free e-books, free skill pills, free webinars, workshops, top tips and so on. This approach may be effective in a direct-to-consumer (D2C) setting; however, within a business-to-business (B2B) marketplace, simply providing free content may not be as beneficial. While it could potentially spark interest among your customer base, it does not guarantee that this engagement will translate into customers being drawn to your services or products. Have you ever been in a position where you have educated the customer, and taught them things, only for them to then go out to RFP, and then you lose the deal? I have, and it hurts big time!

How to build Insight Led Conversations

Depending on how, when and where you are going to open the dialogue with the customer the opening statement/pitch will need to do several things:

1: Demonstrate Credibility
2: Reframe the customer's mind (be disruptive)
3: Address the loss aversion
4: demonstrate the Change behaviour and the change results
5: Answer the Why Us

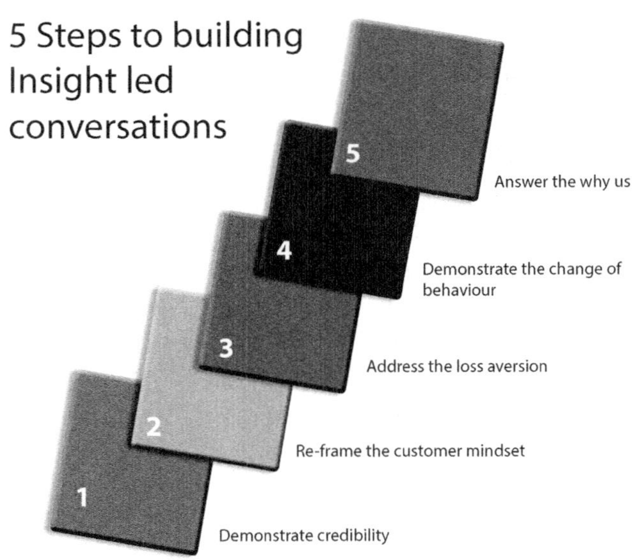

This 5 step approach can work in several different scenarios such as; in conversation, opening statements, in a booked meeting with an existing customer, on an email and so on. In essence, the building blocks follow these 5 core steps. Each can be at different lengths and modified for the occasion, e.g. a short opening statement to engage in a dialogue or delivered through a longer dialogue with existing clients to open the door for deeper conversations.

1: Demonstrate Credibility

When engaging customers in conversations, traditional sales techniques often emphasise quickly initiating conversations with customers and then swiftly moving into the enquiry and discovery phase. However, this approach doesn't work too well today, particularly when the relationship with the customer has not yet been solidified. It's important to recognize that customers may be hesitant to engage in such early interactions. The answer is to start the conversation by sharing some observations about challenges you are seeing and hearing in the marketplace, and preferably some of the things similar companies or people in similar roles are sharing with you.

Starting off your positioning statement by sharing an understanding of a trend or a problem you are observing in the marketplace will immediately begin to establish some rapport and credibility with the customer. You may have some data analysis, market analysis, megatrends or other benchmark data to share at this point, and it is well worth utilising it to establish credibility This should come from your research and insight. It cuts to the chase quite quickly and you should find the customer is a little warmer than leading with a question.

On its own this is not enough to get the customer talking. Because as it hasn't taught them anything apart from you being familiar with the issue or problem. Utilise your research here to ensure you are hot on current issues or trends. Use phrases like:

> *"we are seeing a real trend in the market right now where..."*.
> *"I have been speaking to a lot of (enter job title here) who are sharing with us that ..."*

This probably sounds familiar and is what many people already do as part of the opening statement. However, what usually happens is that they either talk about what their company is doing and why they have built a new product, or they go straight to the question, 'are you seeing that?' It is too early for pitching and too early to ask questions. The customer is still on alert and not ready to engage.

2: Reframe the customers' mind – Be Disruptive

It's crucial to understand that the primary purpose of reframing isn't to present the customer with a solution or to discuss your product's features. Instead, it's about reshaping how the customer perceives a particular problem or trend, prompting them to think more deeply.

To achieve this, your role is to help the customer connect the dots. Introduce them to a fresh perspective that elevates their understanding, revealing a broader issue or opportunity than they initially recognized. The most rewarding response you can hope for after a successful reframe is: "oh, I have never thought about it like that."

This reframe needs to challenge some of their assumptions and must speak directly to their world. Think about the data and insights you can present that will shift their perspective on their business, operations, or competitive stance in the market.

To be able to provide this type of data and insight you will need to know the customers' business better than they do, or at least the part of the business your capabilities are targeted towards. This might sound harsh but you will probably know a lot more about a specific aspect of their business than they do. For example, if you are a company selling HRTech to a car manufacturer you might not know more about car design than the people you are selling to, but you will certainly know more about HR practice, procedures and document management in manufacturing.

To introduce the reframe consider words like:

What may surprise you is…
What some are doing is …
Everybody was wrong when they …
What the market leaders are doing …

Here are some examples of reframes in the conversation:

"Sales leaders often believe that expanding the team is the direct route to increasing sales. But what if I told you that's an expensive and temporary fix? The real game-changer is in investing in a solution that enables your current team to close more deals, faster and more efficiently, maximizing revenue without bloating payroll."

"Consider this: while competitors are burning funds on aggressive recruitment drives, they're missing out on the latent potential of their current teams. What if the real financial edge lies in harnessing this potential through innovative tools, turning every rep into a top performer?"

"It's alarming how many organizations are sinking significant capital into mainstream SaaS platforms, expecting a surge in profitability. But imagine if the secret isn't in the size of the investment but in its strategic placement? The true financial game-changers are those who discern where every dollar can have the most substantial impact."

"Many fear that AI in sales means a loss of personal touch. But what if the true power of AI is in amplifying that personal touch? Imagine a world where AI empowers your team to tailor interactions, anticipate needs, and engage customers in ways that were previously impossible."

You can see that these reframe examples are not telling the customer what the solution is, but is designed to pique their interest, grab their attention and have them think differently.

The key to a truly effective and disruptive reframe is that the customer shouldn't be thinking, 'Yes I totally agree!' or 'That's something that we have been considering'. If they readily accept what you are saying or if they have been thinking along these lines themselves, you are now trying to teach them something they already know and therefore there is nothing unique in your value or proposition. At least not yet. Don't get me wrong it is nice that you are aligned, but the problem is that you haven't managed to demonstrate much value in your reframe.

3: Connect to the Loss Aversion

This is an interesting aspect of positioning and one which many will struggle to do as they often want to get on with the selling. Remember, the key to unlocking bigger sales in a slow economy is not to sell the gain but to focus more on relieving the pain. Loss Aversion reminds us that people are more concerned about losing something than they are about gaining something.

Robert X Cringley, in his book 'Accidental Empires: How the Boys of Silicon Valley Make Their Millions' shares how tech giants, such as IBM used the FUD factor (Fear, Uncertainty and Doubt) to make customers feel uncomfortable or insecure about the current solutions they are using and to lean towards the company spreading the FUD. For you, this means building off the Reframe and getting into the numbers in more detail now.

Combining the FUD factor with Loss Aversion you need to stick to the losses they are experiencing by doing things wrong. Quite often salespeople are equipped with ROI calculators to show the customer the Return on Investment of using their new product or service. Again, this is not the thing you need right now. The Loss isn't about what they could be making, the Loss is what they are currently losing by doing it the way they are doing it.

During the last recession, I worked on a strategies that was highly effective in the legal sector. Here's the example: Law firms maintain libraries (physical and online) to stay updated with the latest legal developments, precedents, and guidelines for case applications. Typically, librarians would subscribe to various publications to ensure their lawyers had comprehensive coverage and resources. However, during the recession, we employed a strategy that highlighted "Loss Aversion." By showing librarians and senior partners that they were often purchasing duplicate information, sometimes even threefold, from different suppliers. By identifying and eliminating this duplicate content, we demonstrated that firms could significantly reduce their expenses. Moreover, by consolidating purchases with fewer suppliers, firms could also benefit from better pricing. Many clients were surprised to discover the extent of their double-spending. As a result, they consolidated their purchases, leading to savings for the firm and increased business for us.

The outcome you are after from this part of the conversation is perhaps disbelief from the customer that they have been wasting so much time, money, resources or whatever you have shown them.

4: Change Behaviour, Transform Results

At last, we're ready to delve into the forward-looking segment where you can guide them towards resolving their issue. Remember, this phase is about addressing the challenge, not highlighting the advantages of choosing you as a supplier. People aren't actively seeking a product or service; they're aiming to resolve their dilemma and rectify the situation you have highlighted up to now.

To truly resonate during this phase, your emphasis should be on the alterations the customer needs to make. Consider the behavioural shifts they must embrace to see different outcomes. When presenting the changes, you can be specific on what needs to change, what capabilities need addressing to solve the puzzle, and how do they go about changing that behaviour, to change the result.

It is going to be very difficult for the seller to resist wandering into features and benefits at this stage but remember the customer must first be open to the concept of change before they can consider partnering with you for that transformation. In essence, you need to lead them to the solution, not with it. How do you do that without talking about the product?

Think of your product or service in 2 different modes: a: What it Does b: How it does it.

To lead the customer to the solution, talk more about the how instead of the what. It is easier for customers to understand and will help remove complexity. They won't be thinking about the interface or colours or button, but more in terms of the operational aspects of the solution.

5: Why Us! – Hypnotic Heartbeat

Having worked through the previous 4 stages this final stage will be the simplest and easiest for the sales person to deliver.

Value propositions come in two kinds, those that attract the left brain thinking, where we create our rational arguments, and those that attract the right brain thinking, where our emotional arguments are conjured up. We've talked earlier about how powerful emotions can be in deciding whether to engage. In Salecology we look at personalities and how they act and react differently, some of which you will see in the Emotional intelligence chapter of this book. For now, we will show you below how to engage both sides of the brain when presenting why to choose you and your solution. Before we do that, I need to share some aspects of psychology on how to engage the brain and put customers into a receptive mindset.

Leading not Pacing

You may have heard of the phrase mirroring, but I want to expand this to matching and mirroring.

Matching is matching the customers' verbal communication style and ensuring that what you say and how you say it matches their style.

Mirroring can establish rapport with the individuals being mirrored. Mirroring the other person's non-verbal gestures such as body language, seating position and stance, makes the person feel a stronger connection to you.

Usually throughout the initial stages of engagement, you should spend time matching and mirroring the customer to establish and build rapport. This is called Pacing, where you are following the customer. Once you have rapport, and find you are mirroring each other, you can start to take the lead and have the customer start to follow your body language and tonal patterns, this is called Leading.

Your positive body language such as nodding and affirming gestures will be important to continue to reinforce the confidence in the solution as you start to share the Why Us.

Removal of Doubt and complexity

Interestingly, we have spent some time taking the customer through several different emotions and rollercoasters, reframing their mind, playing on Loss Aversion, and adding FUD (fear, uncertainty and doubt), but now we need to remove that. You will need to help them in your demonstration, presentation, or summary to remove the complexity from the sale and remove any doubt. Think of the customer having a checklist in their mind and when you present your final solution, they will need to check it off as you go through it. If things are not clear or remain unchecked then don't expect a decision to take place. If you can have them mentally tick it off as you go through your presentation, then their mind can be made up and take the decision to go ahead and engage in the solution.

Hypnotic Language

I have loved the study of hypnotism and enjoy the work of Milton Erikson, Paul McKenna, and the showmanship of Derren Brown. This book isn't going to teach you how to hypnotise your customers into signing orders, that's not ethically acceptable, but it will show you how to use language patterns that hypnotists use and how the power of suggestion works. If you understand that, you can modify the way you present your solutions to gain much better acceptance and have more people say 'Yes' to you.

Unquestionable Truths

The first part of putting someone into an agreeable state is to put the brain into a position where it accepts what is being said is the truth. To do this you must tell it unquestionably true things. A hypnotherapist utilises the Power of 3 to start to put you into a trance state and it follows a pattern as follows:

Step 1: tell the patient 3 unquestionable truths to put their mind into a rest state (stop the inner dialogue from questioning) and then suggest what you want the mind to start to absorb,

Step 2: tell the patient 2 more unquestionable truths, this mixes the suggestion into the camp of the truths,

Step 3: make the repeated suggestion, followed by another truth to embed it.

If performed correctly, with the right amount of confidence and verbal tones, the patient will now be open to suggestion and their mind will be focused on the suggested topic.

The Hypnotic Heartbeat

Linking all the things above, pacing & leading and hypnotic language means you can make benefit statements with more influence to gain customers' approval and confirmation that what they are seeing is useful and adds value to them. Again, depending where you are in the conversation you may be able to add additional information from the conversation and your understanding of the business. If you are still at opening conversations and positioning statements it may be a little harder.

Using the Hypnotic Heartbeat process, you can move the customer into a positive, solution-based mindset that makes them more interested in engaging with the new concepts and ideas. Done correctly, this process removes doubt, questioning, and gets the customer to say yes let's move on with it.

Like an actual human heartbeat, there's an up-and-down flow to the Hypnotic Heartbeat rather than a straight line. This emphasises the tonality you need to use and where the focus of your energy should be.

The process starts with a need you have identified. Here you relay back to the customer what you have established as their need and why they need it.

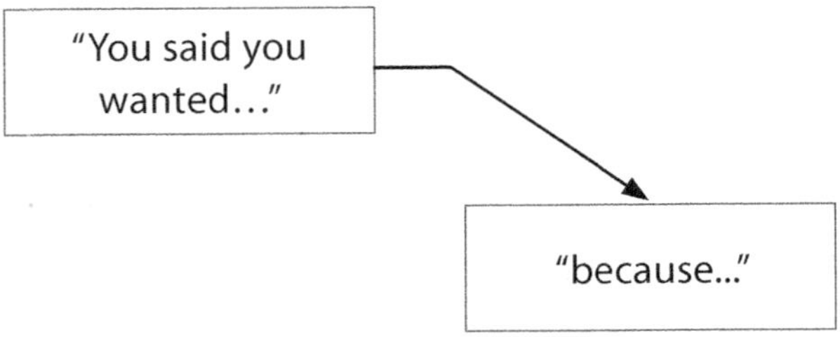

It starts with an opening such as 'you said you wanted to be able to...' This is you replaying their need and reinforcing the fact that they need to do something. Straight after that you reinforce the pains and negative impacts that lead them to want or need it.

Tonality and the Power of 3

It is important to lower your voice when you replay the problems, dissatisfactions, and negative impacts. When people talk about painful things, empathy kicks in and everyone tends to lower their voice and demonstrates some mutual concern. As you get into the reaffirmation of the need and why they need it, utilise the power of 3, and replay two or three things about what they have said about the problem and impact. This therefore becomes unquestionable because you are only replaying what they have said to you.

Don't stop midway!

Don't go off on a tangent at this point. Some people ask a question at this point to try and gain confirmation that this is correct – don't! If you stop after the pain aspects, you will take the customer back to a more inquisitive mindset and they may now start talking about painful things or reliving the issues and you will be into the explore / discovery aspect of the sale. Which is not where you want to be right now.

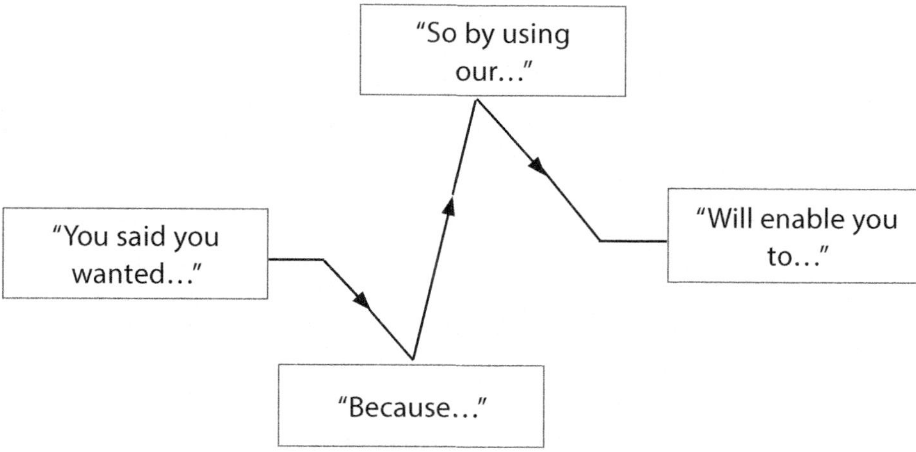

Don't skip a beat

The third step is to bounce upward with your tonal patterns, energy, and volume. This is setting the scene of the happier place to be, the answer to their needs, by telling them the how you solve the problem.

This, as you saw in the hypnotic language paragraph, is the moment you are making the suggestion – "So by using our …..".

You also saw in the hypnotic language that you need to follow up again with some more truths for the brain to accept the sequence. This is where you follow up with the benefits already uncovered during you value questions and positive impact questions.

> "So, by using our … will enable you to … "

The tonal pattern in the benefit statements comes back to neutral. The ear will pick up on the tonal level and it will reinforce the confidence and stability in the benefits. To ensure these stick, remember the power of 3 – you should be able to reinforce the benefits with more than a one liner, present back 3 benefits to enforce the impact of the solution.

Confirmation and Gaining Buy-in

To complete the cycle, we need the customer to confirm in their mind that they agree with the statement. This verbal confirmation is much more than confirming that you have got it right. If the customer says out loud that they agree, understand why you are recommending it, it tells their mind that this is correct and turns off the inner voice of doubt.

Continuous Evolution

Having explored the importance of challenging the status quo and the psychological barriers that often stand in the way, it's now time to delve into the heart of what sets successful technology businesses apart: Continuous Evolution. This is both from a company-wide perspective as well as the sales organisation.

In such a dynamic environment, resting on past successes is not just detrimental; it's fatal. As a sales leader, you must recognize that what worked yesterday might not work tomorrow. The strategies that brought in customers last year might be obsolete next year. But continuous evolution isn't just about reacting to change; it's about anticipating it. It's about being proactive, staying ahead of the curve, and leading the market rather than just following it.

You Can't Afford to Stand Still

Customer Expectations are Evolving:
Today's customers are tech-savvy, informed, and have a plethora of options at their fingertips. With every new product or feature they encounter, their expectations shift. They're not just looking for a product; they're seeking solutions that evolve with their growing needs. As Brian Halligan, CEO of HubSpot, mentions in "Inbound Marketing," the way people buy has changed, and as a result, the way we sell must transform too.

The Competitive Landscape is Shifting:
In SaaS, new players emerge every day, each bringing fresh ideas, innovative solutions, and aggressive sales strategies. Continuous evolution ensures you maintain your competitive edge, differentiating your offerings and value proposition.

Technological Advancements Wait for No One:
The pace of technological change is relentless. New tools, platforms, and integrations are constantly being developed. By ensuring continuous evolution, you harness these advancements, integrating them into your offerings and sales strategies.

Crafting a Strategy for Continuous Evolution

Understanding the importance of evolution is one thing; implementing it is another. So, how can sales organisations ensure that continuous evolution is not just a buzzword but a deeply ingrained principle?

Firstly, it is to realise that driving a more disruptive mindset is an organisational thing and a team sport, it is not merely up to sales to go it alone. You need the organisation to get behind sharing knowledge, sharing insight to enable the sales team to be able to construct conversations with customers around it. Where many sales organisations have failed in the past, is expecting the team on their own to be able to miraculously conjure up insights.

Commercial Knowledge and Product Knowledge

From experience, the sales team are taught Features and Benefits, but in reality, it is nothing of the sort. They are normally trained in features and functionality. It often sounds like this:

> *here is a dashboard (features) it shows the following pieces of information (feature), it can be modified to show the following pieces of information (Feature / functionality), you can make it you home screen (feature) so it comes up when you login in (functionality). We also have a Single Sign On (Feature) saving you time from having multiple logins (functionality hoping to be a benefit).*

Of course, we do need to train the team on functionality and for them to understand how the product works, but the real skill will be teaching the team why the functionality was built into the software. The programmers and product development team made some decisions in compiling the features and functionality. It would have come down to;

- No one else is doing this (Unique selling point)
- This is different from what everyone else is doing (distinctive selling point)
- Everyone else is doing this (common tools that just need to be there)

Having uncovered the unique and distinctive selling points, now educate the sales team on why we are doing it like this, and why it will make a difference to the potential customers. This training is so much more beneficial than reeling off what it does by focusing much more on the why it does it.

Teaching the Why, enables the sales team to be more persuasive and build commercial knowledge into their everyday pitch. They start to become more focused on changing the way people do things, rather than selling products and services.

Be Informed

Knowledge is power. Sales Professionals must immerse themselves in the ever-evolving industry and landscape. This means not just being aware of industry trends but understanding their implications. Regularly reading industry journals, attending webinars, and participating in forums can provide invaluable insights. Authors like Neil Patel and Sujan Patel, known for their expertise in SaaS growth strategies, offer a wealth of knowledge through their writings and talks. You have bought this book to increase your knowledge, but you will be surprised how many other people fail to enhance their knowledge by staying informed of what is happening in their market, industry or profession.

Continuous Learning

A sales team's skills and knowledge are its most valuable assets. Regular training sessions, workshops, and certifications ensure that they're equipped to navigate the world around them. It is commonplace for sales managers and leaders to bring in people from the business to provide knowledge and education to the team. Marketing will come along and share the new campaigns, product teams will come and share about roadmaps and releases, and sales enablement perhaps do a workshop and some skills development piece. But ask yourself this question - what are you doing about enhancing their knowledge of the SaaS market space, technology advancements and commercial teaching?

Feedback as a Guiding Light

Your customers are on the front lines, using your product daily. A great source of insider knowledge is from them. Their feedback is an invaluable resource, offering insights into areas of improvement, unmet needs, and emerging trends. Engaging in regular dialogues with customers, understanding their challenges, and seeking their feedback can provide a roadmap for evolution.

Embracing a Growth Mindset of Continuous Improvement: Sales strategies must be regularly reviewed, analysed, and refined. This iterative process ensures that strategies are not just reactive but proactive, anticipating changes and capitalizing on emerging opportunities. Utilise sales meetings, 121s and sales accompaniments to continuously reflect on what is working and what could we do even better. If you record sales calls, presentations, and demonstrations, don't be afraid to listen to the call as a group and spot areas that would make it better.

Ask the team to present their sales presentations to the team, for won and or lost deals, so everyone can learn from it. This type of culture needs to be safe, it is not about crucifying the salesperson, it is about continuous improvement.

We instigated a call-listening culture into a Business Intelligence company, where the CEO, CFO, CTO among others had to listen to at least 5-10 calls per week, recordings mainly, and provide feedback to the individuals. This was not easy to do, as time is always short and priorities constantly changing, however, the benefits gained from it were immense. Product development improved, value propositions improved and the insight these leaders gave the individuals, were gold nuggets of how to pinpoint more accurately the disrupters and reframes needed to engage the customer. This also helped share with the wider sales team better angles to Challenge the Status Quo.

Conclusion

Continuous evolution is the lifeblood of sales success. It's a journey of relentless growth, learning, and transformation. As you navigate the challenging economic conditions of today's market, remember that evolution is not just a strategy, it's a mindset. It's about seeing change not as a challenge but as an opportunity, an opportunity to redefine the rules, set new benchmarks, and achieve unparalleled success.

The Power of Vision

In the journey of challenging the status quo and fostering a culture of continuous evolution, there's an essential compass that guides every step: Vision. It's the beacon that illuminates the path, the rallying cry that unites and motivates, and the foundation upon which disruptive success is built.

Why Vision Matters

Every transformative journey begins with a destination in mind – aka The Vision. It's the overarching goal, the grand ambition, the picture of success. But why is vision so crucial?

Direction:	A clear vision provides direction. It offers a roadmap, guiding the organization through the complexities of the market, ensuring every decision and every strategy aligns with the end goal.
Motivation:	Vision is the fuel that drives motivation. It's the promise of a better future, a world where the organization's offerings redefine norms, set benchmarks, and achieve unparalleled success. This promise inspires, motivates, and propels the team forward, even in the face of challenges.
Differentiation:	In a crowded market, a compelling vision sets an organization apart. It's the unique value proposition, the promise that resonates with customers, making them not just buyers but believers.

The Interplay of Vision and Disruptive Mindset

A disruptive mindset, as previously discussed, is about challenging norms, questioning the familiar, and seeking transformative solutions. But this mindset, in isolation, can be directionless. It's the vision that gives it purpose, channelling the disruptive energy towards a defined goal.

However, having a vision is just the starting point. It's the conviction in this vision, the unwavering belief in its possibility, that truly empowers a disruptive mindset. When you have a vision but also an opinion about its transformative potential, it instils confidence. It sends a powerful message to customers: "We're not just offering a product; we're championing a change. And we believe, unequivocally, in the potential of this change."

Crafting and Communicating the Vision

Having a vision is one thing; effectively communicating it is another. Here's how you can craft and convey a compelling vision:

Clarity: A vision should be clear and concise. It should encapsulate the essence of the organization's ambitions in a manner that's easily understood and resonates deeply.

Inclusivity: While the vision might originate at the top, it's essential to involve the entire organization in its refinement. This inclusivity ensures buy-in, fostering a sense of collective ownership.

Consistent Communication: The vision should be consistently communicated across all channels, be it internal meetings, customer interactions, or marketing campaigns. Regular reminders reinforce its importance, keeping it at the forefront of all endeavours.

Living the Vision: It's not enough to just talk about the vision; it must be lived. Every decision, every strategy and every interaction should reflect the vision, making it an integral part of the organization's DNA.

As an MBA student, I spent a lot of time learning about the power of vision and mission statements, especially from the likes of modern management authority Peter Drucker, and I still hear references to BHAGs, big hairy audacious goals, which I first read in Jim Collins and Jerry I. Porras's book "Built to Last". Albeit I think the A has taken a new form in the current vernacular. One of the things we also discussed is the power of everyone working towards a particular goal or mission of the organisation, but in today's world I think we need to realise that individuals need to have their own Vision, preferably linked to the organisation, but if they are truly going to be disruptive, they need to have an opinion.

The Salesperson's Vision - Revolutionising the Market Space

In the bustling corridors of software and tech businesses, amidst the hum of innovation and the rhythm of relentless ambition, there's a force often overlooked but profoundly impactful: the individual vision of the salesperson/account manager. This isn't about targets, quotas, or even the broader organizational goals. This is about the personal, deeply held belief of each salesperson about how they can reshape the market, challenge norms, and introduce transformative solutions.

The Visionary Salesperson

Every successful salesperson enters the field with more than just a product to sell, they carry with them a vision. This vision is their unique perspective on how their product or service can redefine the market, solve pressing challenges, and usher in a new era of possibilities. It's this vision that differentiates a salesperson from being just a representative of a company to becoming a market influencer.

For a salesperson, their vision is their narrative. It's the story they tell their clients, not just about the product but about the future. It's the promise of a world where challenges are addressed more efficiently, where operations are smoother, and where growth is not just possible but inevitable.

Crafting a Personal Vision

The journey to becoming a visionary salesperson begins with introspection. It's about understanding one's beliefs about the market, recognizing the gaps, and visualizing the transformative potential of the solutions they offer. This isn't a one-time exercise but a continuous process of refinement as they gain more insights from the field.

But how does a salesperson translate this vision into actionable strategies? Opposite are 4 key things to consider when building a personal vision:

1: Introspection and Self-awareness

Every vision starts from within. For a salesperson, this means understanding their intrinsic motivations, strengths, and values. What aspects of the industry resonate most with them? What change do they wish to see or drive in their domain? By reflecting on these questions, a salesperson begins to shape the contours of their vision.

2. Understanding the Market Narrative

A vision isn't crafted in isolation; it's rooted in the realities of the market. This involves understanding the current market narrative. What are the prevailing beliefs and trends? Where does the market seem to be headed, and where does it actually need to go? By juxtaposing these insights with personal beliefs, a salesperson can craft a vision that's both personal and relevant.

3. Positioning as a Thought Leader

A vision gains weight when it's backed by knowledge and expertise. For a salesperson, this means continuously striving to be a thought leader in their domain. This doesn't just involve understanding the product they're selling but also the broader industry trends, challenges, and innovations. Positioning themselves as experts, salespeople also lend credibility to their vision by sharing insights, writing articles, or even engaging in discussions, they position themselves as individuals who have a deep understanding of the market and its future.

4. Building Authentic Relationships

A vision is not just a personal roadmap; it's also a narrative shared with clients. And for this narrative to resonate, it needs to be rooted in authenticity. This means building genuine relationships with clients, understanding their challenges, and aligning the vision to address these challenges. It's about showcasing not just the product's value but also the transformative potential of the vision behind it.

Not included in the above 4, but part of the subtext is the idea of Continuous Learning. For a salesperson's vision to remain relevant, they need to be in a state of continuous learning. This ensures that their vision is not just based on personal beliefs but is also backed by industry knowledge. We covered this in the previous chapter, but will also dig deeper in the Insight Agility section of the book.

The Ripple Effect of a Visionary Salesperson

When a salesperson operates with a clear vision, the impact is profound. They don't just meet targets, they change mindsets. They introduce clients to new possibilities, challenge them to think bigger and inspire them to be part of a transformative journey.

Moreover, this vision has a ripple effect. It influences colleagues, reshapes sales strategies, and even impacts product development. It ensures that the organisation is not just reacting to market demands but is proactively shaping them.

In the competitive world of sales, competition is fierce and the pace relentless, it's the visionaries who stand out. They are the torch-bearers of change, the pioneers of transformation, and the architects of the future. As you navigate the challenges of today's market, remember that it's not just about selling a product; it's about selling a vision. And in this vision lies the power to disrupt and revolutionize the market space.

Conclusion

As we conclude our exploration of the Disruptive Mindset, it's essential to recognize that this mindset is more than just a business strategy, it's a transformative approach that reshapes how we view challenges and opportunities. Embracing a disruptive mindset means continually questioning the status quo, seeking innovative solutions, and being unafraid to pivot or make bold moves when necessary. It's about fostering a culture of continuous learning and adaptation, where creativity and innovation are not just encouraged but are integral to the organization's DNA.

The Disruptive Mindset is not a one-time initiative but an ongoing journey. It requires a commitment to perpetual growth, learning, and the courage to take calculated risks. By embedding this mindset into the core of your business strategy, you position your company not just to survive but to thrive and lead in an ever-evolving market.

As we transition from the realm of embracing disruption to mastering the art of agility in insights, we carry forward the principles of innovation and adaptability. The next force, Insight Agility, builds upon the foundation laid by a Disruptive Mindset, taking us deeper into the tactical execution of these innovative strategies.

2

Force 2: Insight Agility

2

Ia

Contents

Insightful Agility

In a world where market conditions shift rapidly and customer 'needs' evolve almost overnight, success isn't just about having the best product or the most efficient processes. It's about possessing the agility to adapt swiftly to these changes, but not just any agility—Insightful Agility. This is the ability to make quick decisions and pivot strategies based on deep insights, ensuring that every move is calculated, strategic, and aligned with both current realities and future possibilities. But how can a tech business cultivate this blend of agility and insight, especially in an uncertain economic environment?

There are a few things that you should consider when building insight agility:

Data-Driven Decision Making
We are in the age of big data and therefore businesses have access to a wealth of information about their users, market trends, and competitive landscape. Insightful Agility hinges on harnessing this data, analysing it for actionable insights, and using it to inform strategic decisions. It's about moving beyond gut feelings to decisions rooted in concrete evidence.

Staying Ahead of Market Shifts
In many cases the market is characterized by its rapid shifts, new technologies, emerging competitors and changing customer preferences. Businesses with Insightful Agility need to anticipate the shifts and by keeping a finger on the pulse of the industry and staying informed about potential disruptors, they position themselves to be proactive rather than reactive.

Pivoting Strategies
A strategy that worked yesterday might not be effective tomorrow. Insightful Agility involves regularly revisiting and reassessing strategies, being willing to pivot when necessary, and ensuring that execution is swift and efficient. It's about fostering a culture where change is embraced, and adaptability is valued.

Continuous Learning and Evolution
The tech landscape is a continuous learning curve. Businesses that prioritize learning—whether it's about new technologies, market dynamics, or customer needs—position themselves for sustained success. Insightful Agility is about cultivating a mindset of continuous evolution, ensuring that the business remains relevant and competitive.

In the previous chapter, Disruptive Mindset, we discussed in depth the need for insight and using it to reframe the mind of the customer. The challenge of course is how to build Insight and how to utilise it.

In this section of the book, we will look at some core building blocks to help you implement this into your organisation.

Building an Insight Factory	How and where can you garner insight, how do you ensure it is captured, and who does the analysis?
Packaging Insight	How do you package the insight for it to be understood and applied in various aspects of the sales cycle?
Continuous Learning	How do you instil a learning culture to develop Agility, curiosity and resilience, enabling the team to constantly evolve their approach?

Along with the items listed, we will also look at the agile approach and how to utilise proactive problem solving.

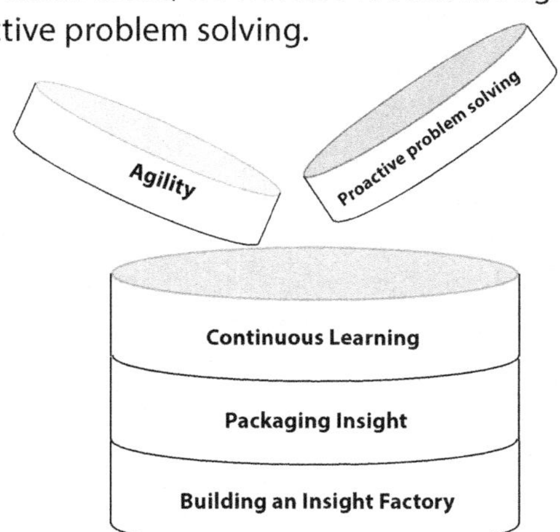

Building An Insight Factory

The first challenge of building an insightful sales organisation is to understand where insight comes from and who possesses it? Is there a particular department that is responsible for being the insight generation machine or is it everybody's responsibility? It is easy to say that everyone is responsible for bringing and building insight, but really? Is everybody responsible for it? Insight is not a new idea, but sales teams and businesses have struggled to work out how to get 'Insight' into the hands of those who need it. Equally, they often feel it is something that just happens. From experience, I have seen so many organisations hear a good piece of insight and it is grabbed with both hands by the sales team and used on every sales call. While this is good, it isn't great, that piece of insight isn't necessarily right for every customer.

In the age of digital transformation, data is abundant. But raw data, in isolation, is like an untold story. It holds potential, but its true value is unlocked only when it's interpreted, understood, and acted upon.

For sales organisations, this means equipping your sales team with the right tools and training to harness this data effectively. It's about moving beyond surface-level metrics to deep, actionable insights. By understanding market shifts, recognizing emerging trends, and anticipating potential challenges, you position yourself not just to respond to the market but to shape it.

Imagine if you had a sales strategy so attuned to the market that it can predict customer needs even before they arise. This is the power of data-driven decisions. It's not about reacting to the past, it's about forecasting the future.

An Insight Factory is more than just a collection of tools and training, it's a holistic system designed to transform raw data into actionable insights. Here's how you can build and optimize your very own Insight Factory.

Centralised Data Repository

Begin by consolidating all your data sources into a centralized repository. Whether it's CRM data, website analytics, customer feedback, or third-party market research, ensure that all data streams flow into a single, accessible hub. This not only streamlines data access but also ensures consistency and accuracy.

In many organisations, data is scattered across various platforms, tools, and systems. The challenge is not just collecting this data, but organizing it in a way that's accessible, consistent, and actionable. This is where a centralised data repository comes into play.

Before diving into the 'how', it's crucial to understand the 'why'. A centralized data repository:

Eliminates Silos:	Data silos can hinder cross-functional collaboration and lead to inconsistent or even contradictory insights. Centralization ensures everyone is on the same page.
Enhances Efficiency:	With data in one place, teams can quickly access the information they need without having to jump between systems.
Ensures Data Integrity:	A unified repository reduces the risk of data duplication, discrepancies, and errors.

Consider a centralized data repository as a strategic asset not just a storage solution. By consolidating data, sales organizations can derive holistic insights, make informed decisions, and drive cohesive strategies that resonate with the market's pulse. It's the first, crucial step in transforming raw data into a powerful force for growth and innovation.

Steps to Build a Centralised Data Repository

1.	**Audit Existing Data Sources:**	Start by identifying all the data sources within your organization. This could include CRMs, sales tools, website analytics, customer feedback platforms, and third-party research.
2.	**Define Data Standards:**	Establish clear standards for data entry, naming conventions, and formats. This ensures consistency and reduces the risk of errors or discrepancies.
3.	**Choose the Right Platform:**	Depending on the volume and complexity of your data, you might opt for a data warehouse, a cloud-based storage solution, or a dedicated data management platform. Ensure the platform is scalable, secure, and integrates well with other tools in your tech stack.
4.	**Implement Data Integration Tools:**	Use ETL (Extract, Transform, Load) tools to automate the process of pulling data from various sources, transforming it into a consistent format, and loading it into the repository.
5.	**Ensure Data Security**	Protecting your data is paramount. Implement robust security measures, including encryption, access controls, and regular backups.
6.	**Regularly Clean and Update Data:**	Data can become outdated or redundant over time. Schedule regular data cleaning sessions to remove duplicates, correct errors, and update records.
7.	**Review & Evolve:**	Technology and business needs evolve. Regularly review your data repository setup, making adjustments as needed to accommodate new data sources, tools, or organizational objectives.

Salespeople won't really analyse the data!

This book is not the 'by the book' approach, it is about what really works rather than what should work. Yes, it would be ideal to equip your sales team with cutting-edge analytics tools that allow them to sift through data, identify patterns, and derive insights. You could invest in advanced analytic tools that offer predictive analytics, trend analysis, and visualisation capabilities with the goal of making data interpretation intuitive and actionable. The truth is, invest all the money you like, the bulk of the team will not do the analysis.

You need data analysts and cross-functional teams such as the product team and marketing to do the heavy lifting and start to pull together and derive insights. But sales do need to input into this mechanism.

Feedback and Customer knowledge

In many organisations product development and marketing are often frustrated at the lack of knowledge sharing that comes back from the sales team. These two departments are thirsty for what the prospects and customers think. To be frank, the way to get the salespeople to capture and provide this insight is to demonstrate that it is beneficial to the seller, not just a chore, and make it easy to capture and easy to share.

Think of it in terms of the things that are important to the sales team, will it:

Shorten Sales Cycles:	By understanding customer preferences and behaviours, salespeople will be able to tailor their pitches more effectively.
Increase Close Rates:	Insights can reveal objections or concerns that prospects might have, allowing them to address them proactively.
Enhance Customer Relationships:	By demonstrating a deep understanding of customer needs, salespeople can position themselves as trusted advisors rather than just vendors.

These things sound good, but will it, and does it, really do that? The answer is yes, but the sceptical salesperson will possibly not see it that way. The winning formula will be to pinpoint real-world examples of why that piece of insight or knowledge would have fast-tracked the deal or expedited the sale. The easier you make it for salespeople to capture and share insights, the more likely they are to do it.

The first step is to utilise the tools that integrate seamlessly with the platforms they already use, like your CRM or communication apps. Find ways to capture items into the CRM that will be easy to find and regurgitate during or after the sale.

We are now in a world where we have access to AI-driven tools that can automatically capture insights from sales calls, emails, and/or meetings. From my current experience, teams are still finding their ways around how to implement and use them but call listening and call tracking are making it so much easier to analyse the data and provide feedback on a lot more than just sentiment.

The easiest way to get knowledge and insight sharing to happen is to create an environment where it is part of the everyday conversation and when it is shared it is celebrated. Here are some quick wins to introduce insight-sharing in your everyday conversations:

Team Meetings	In the weekly or monthly sales meetings encourage sharing experiences, challenges and insights. By that I mean carve out time in the agenda for people to present a case example and learnings.
Deal Clinics	Capture in the deal clinics reasons why the customer is interested in the solution. Consider the 3 Whys: why are the changing from what they are already doing, why are they interested now, and why are they talking to us?
Deal reviews	Build regular deal reviews to pull out insights into win/loss analysis. Again this is a deeper version of the team meeting, and consider bringing in other departments to listen to the review.

Incentivise	Offer incentives or recognition for those who consistently contribute valuable insight. Remember the phrase: what gets measured gets done, what gets rewarded gets done first!

Double Loop Learning and Feedback

Double-loop learning, also known as double-loop feedback, is a concept in organisational learning and personal development. It refers to the ability to question and modify the underlying assumptions and values that inform our actions, rather than just the actions themselves. This concept was introduced by Chris Argyris, a business theorist, in the context of organisational behaviour and learning.

The term "double loop" in "double-loop learning" refers to the two distinct loops or processes involved in this type of learning.

First Loop (Single-loop Learning): This loop involves detecting and correcting errors in a way that leaves the underlying beliefs and assumptions unchanged. It's about making adjustments to actions and behaviours without questioning the reasons behind them. In this loop, the focus is on "doing things right" based on existing policies, goals, or values.

Second Loop (Double-loop Learning): This loop goes beyond just correcting errors in actions and behaviours. It delves deeper to question and potentially modify the underlying beliefs, values, and assumptions that led to those actions in the first place. In this loop, the focus shifts to "doing the right things," which might involve changing the fundamental rules, policies, or objectives based on new insights.

The "double" in "double-loop" signifies the addition of this second loop, which is an extra layer of reflection and inquiry that goes beyond the immediate correction of errors. It's about understanding the deeper "why" behind actions and decisions, not just the "what" or "how." In essence, while single-loop learning is about working within the existing system and making improvements, double-loop learning challenges and potentially changes the system itself.

To understand double-loop learning, it's helpful to contrast it with single-loop learning:

1. **Single-loop Learning**: This is where individuals, teams, or organizations modify their actions according to the difference between expected and obtained outcomes. It's akin to a thermostat that learns when it needs to turn on or off based on the difference between the actual temperature and the desired temperature. However, it doesn't question why that temperature is desired in the first place.

2. **Double-loop Learning**: This goes a step further. Instead of just adjusting actions, it questions the underlying assumptions and beliefs that lead to those actions. Using the thermostat analogy, it would be like questioning why we set the temperature to a certain level and whether there's a better temperature setting that might be more energy-efficient or comfortable.

From an organizational context, and to put this into context for us in this book, double-loop learning can be transformative. For example:

- **Single-loop**: A company might notice that a product is not selling well, so they increase their marketing efforts.

- **Double-loop**: The same company might question why the product was developed in the first place, whether it truly meets customer needs, or if there's a fundamental flaw in their product development process.

I think you probably see the inference in double-loop learning and feedback. In a sales context, double-loop feedback involves not only addressing the immediate challenges or discrepancies in sales outcomes but also examining and potentially revising the underlying assumptions, strategies, and beliefs that guide the sales process. Here's how double-loop feedback can be applied in sales:

Identify the Discrepancy: This is the starting point for both single-loop and double-loop learning. For instance, a sales team might notice that they are not meeting their sales targets for a particular product.

1. **Single-loop Response**: The immediate response might be to provide additional training to the sales team, offer promotions to customers, or increase advertising spend.

2. **Double-loop Inquiry**: Instead of stopping at the immediate response, the sales team or management would delve deeper to question the foundational beliefs and assumptions. Some questions that might arise include:

   - Is our sales strategy aligned with current market trends?
   - Are we targeting the right customer segments?
   - Is there a fundamental mismatch between our product and market needs?
   - Are our sales targets realistic given the market conditions?
   - Are there organizational or cultural issues affecting sales performance?

3. **Revising Assumptions**: Based on the insights from the double-loop inquiry, the sales team might realize that they need to pivot their strategy. For instance, they might discover that their product is better suited for a different customer segment than they initially believed.

4. **Implementing Changes**: Once the underlying assumptions are revised, the sales team can implement changes. This might involve retraining the team to approach a new customer segment, rebranding the product, or even revising the product based on market feedback.

5. **Feedback and Iteration**: The process doesn't stop after implementing changes. The sales team would continue to gather feedback, monitor sales outcomes, and periodically engage in double-loop learning to ensure that their strategies and assumptions remain relevant.

Double-loop learning and double-loop feedback are essential for challenging the assumptions and not simply trying to fix the symptom, but actually looking for something that is the cause or some other aspects that are affecting it.

When having discussions with the sales team about deal reviews, or team meetings, it is imperative that you utilise a double-loop approach to dig deeper and to think more widely than the initial problem. This helps garner deeper insight into the solutions being offered to the customer and also helps challenge assumptions and the status quo.

Benefits of Double-Loop Feedback:

Adaptability:	Sales teams become more agile and adaptable to changing market conditions.
Sustainable Growth:	By addressing root causes rather than just symptoms, sales teams can achieve more sustainable growth.
Improved Morale:	Understanding and addressing deeper issues can lead to better morale and motivation among salespeople.
Innovation:	Questioning foundational beliefs can lead to innovative sales strategies and approaches.

Utilising Double Loop should stop you from looking one-dimensionally at the problem and start to build agility into your thinking.

PESTEL Analysis

Understanding the client isn't just about knowing their immediate needs. It's about understanding the larger macro environment they operate within. Top sales people, and sales organisations, need to ensure that they have strong market and industry knowledge. This is where the PESTEL analysis shines, offering salespeople a strategic lens to view potential challenges and opportunities in their market.

Introduced by Harvard Professor Francis J. Aguilar, in his 1967 book Scanning the Business Environment, A PESTEL Analysis enables you to look at a company or industry across a multitude of factors and helps you gain a good overview of the marketplace, what things are affecting the business right now, what is presenting opportunities and potential challenges.

PESTEL stands for Political, Economic, Sociocultural, Technological, Environmental, and Legal. This framework helps you analyse external macro-environmental factors that might impact their product's appeal and the company's operation in a particular region, market or industry. (See overleaf)

Utilise the acronym when conducting your research. Take each letter and consider what is happening in that area to get a strong understanding of the customer and 'put yourself in their shoes'. This will provide you a strong position to engage with some background knowledge and an idea of why they should talk to you.

Once you are engaging with the customer you will need more information to be able to start to look for greater synergies and align your product and services to their business goals and objectives. So, it will also be worth looking at their website for any strategic objectives, current initiatives, company goals and aspirations, and news articles etc.

The insights garnered from the PESTEL analysis make it simpler and easier for salespeople to see the advantages of gaining insight and allow them to tailor opening statements and sales pitches, as well as proactively identify potential objections and pricing issues.

Political:	Government stability, trade restrictions, and data protection laws. Sales Implication: If you're selling a SaaS product, understanding data protection laws in your client's country can help you position your product's compliance as a strong selling point.
Economic:	Overall economic health, inflation rates, and exchange rate fluctuations. Sales Implication: In an economic downturn, emphasize the cost-saving benefits of your product or offer flexible pricing.
Sociocultural:	Population demographics, cultural attitudes towards technology, and work culture. Sales Implication: For a company that values traditional face-to-face meetings, highlight how your software solution can mimic this personal touch.
Technological:	Infrastructure, tech adoption rates, and R&D activity in the industry. Sales Implication: If a potential client's infrastructure is dated, focus on the ease of integration and low tech requirements of your solution.
Environmental:	Environmental regulations, sustainability concerns, and climate. Sales Implication: If your company practices green computing, it could be a pivotal selling point for eco-conscious clients.
Legal Factors:	Employment laws, health and safety, and industry-specific regulations. Sales Implication: Understanding legal constraints can prevent unwanted surprises post-sale and build trust with prospects.

Packaging Insight

Gathering insight is one thing, packaging it into usable data to help 'Go To Market' is another. As we spoke about in the Insight Factory chapter, salespeople typically won't analyse the information unless we show them the power or benefits of it. Too often we inundate them with intelligence, but they end up drowning in it and don't know what to do with it.

The real power of the insight is to look at it, understand it, then package it and present it back into how it can be applied. This works in several formats but to ensure that it is used correctly we need to consider the chapter earlier about challenging the status quo, and how the sales team are going to be able to articulate the insight when engaging with the customer. We should also consider how different messages will also be attached to this.

FABs

This book isn't about sales 101 but I wanted to reference a couple of key things to consider before we get deeper into how to package insight and that starts by reminding ourselves about Features, Advantages and Benefits.

The concept of "Features, Advantages, and Benefits" (FAB) was first introduced by Theodore Leavitt, a marketing professor at Harvard Business School, in the 1960s. He developed the FAB framework to help companies improve their marketing and sales messaging by focusing on the value that a product or service offers to customers. However, in his framework, he was using Advantages as a competitive advantage or the positive aspects of the features that make the product or service better than alternatives.

Tom Hopkins modified advantages in his 1980 book How to Master the Art of Selling, in which he broke down the features of the product or service into advantages, which are the positive aspects of those features, and then into benefits, which are the specific ways in which the product or service will improve the customer's life or solve a problem. By presenting the benefits in a clear and compelling way, salespeople can help potential customers understand why the product or service is worth buying, and overcome objections based on cost or other factors. Here is a quick breakdown for you.

Features

Features are characteristics of your product or service. It is what the product has or does and they are easy to talk about, for example features of an iPhone are the super high-quality camera, iMessage, Facetime and the iOS operating system. Features are not only linked to products, for example, some organisations are more service lead so it could be features such as lead times, the innovation team, the depth of coverage and so on. For software and tech solutions you could also include functionality in this category.

Advantages

Advantages are how the product can help - anyone. As said earlier this is how the features can help people in general. Advantage statements typically come in the format of "because of (insert feature) you can do (insert advantage)". They are more persuasive than features, especially at the beginning of the sales cycle, but as the sales cycle progresses, advantage statements have a reduced impact on influencing the customer. Customers might be interested to hear how others have used the product, and how it has helped them, but very quickly they are more interested in how it might meet their own requirements.

The marketing materials will call them 'benefits' but in reality you now know them as Advantages because they are generic and not tailored to each specific prospect or customer.

Benefits

As we have now established Benefits are how a product or service meets the customer's expressed needs. Demonstrating Benefits is the most influential and powerful behaviour a salesperson can exhibit.

USPs or DSPs

Selling used to be about sharing with customers your USPs, your unique selling points, but as the world becomes smaller, and the speed of product development increases, it is becoming tougher to differentiate products and create truly unique features. Added on to that, the internet has made customers believe that whatever you are selling they can probably buy somewhere else and probably cheaper, whether this is true or not. Features, however, do not have to be USP's they can also be DSP's, distinctive selling points.

Unique Selling Point (USP)	What your product or company does differently that makes it unique
Distinctive Selling Point (DSP)	Things your product or company does better than others

Distinctive selling points are aspects that your company, product or collection of features can do better than the competition. Taking the mobile phone again as an example, when the iPhone launched it most definitely wasn't the best phone on the market, it wasn't the first to have a touchscreen, it wasn't the first to play music and it wasn't the first to be able to browse the internet. The market leader at that time was Nokia, who brought out the Nokia N95 to stop Apple in its tracks. Designed to be the most powerful phone on the market, cheaper than the new market entry from Apple, and designed to have all the latest features plus more. However the iPhone made its product more distinctive. It looked different to everyone else, they advertised it differently to everyone else, and homed in on making it cool and fashionable rather than all about technical specifications and features.

Building the Insight Gameplan

Having defined features, advantages and benefits, consideration needs to be applied to whether the insight leads the customer to one of your Distinctive Selling Points or starts to create a Unique Value Proposition. It doesn't matter which one, it simply matters that it leads the customer to a solution you can provide.

To package the insight correctly we can build a gameplan that will help the sale progress in the right direction, leading the customer to the solution as opposed to the salesperson leading with the solution.

To do so we must accept something that flies in the face of what salespeople, and often managers believe they do; solution selling. Most salespeople that sold SaaS, Tech or any other type of B2B system over the past 30 years consider themselves to be consultants or a solution seller, they go on solution-selling training courses where they learn SPIN or BANT type of training, but let's be honest the salesperson isn't a 'Consultative Seller'. Yes, they do consult, as in they ask questions and deep dive to uncover needs and explore the pains and gains so they can demonstrate an ROI (return on investment). But, come on, let's be honest, they are trying to sell the packaged service that is on offer. Yes, maybe some different menu options with different pricing but ultimately a uniform platform with some upsell elements, but they are not really going to create a new product to solve the customers requirement.

The good news is that our sales people have:

1: Defined Target Audience and Segment
The sales team do not start with a blank slate, marketing and the sales strategy should have already defined the client base, segments, and target audiences within it.

2: Predetermined set of hypotheses that the customer is struggling with
The product and services have been defined to already solve a number of issues and therefore the salesperson doesn't need to diagnose each customer's individual needs from the start. Yes, the conversation in a live setting will take different turns and the salesperson needs to react to the questions they ask and deal with different objections and questions raised. However, the initial opening statements and hypothesis are pre-set prior to the call and the advantage and benefit statements are already in place.

3: Packaged solutions with measurable impact
The burden of building a bespoke solution for the salesperson has already been removed and the customer will potentially have a few tailored or customised options to make it feel individualised. Case studies, proven metrics and outcomes have already been captured to add credence to the proposition.

All this said, let me be fair, the salesperson still has a job to do, it is far from transactional selling, but it is not as complex as the 'solution selling' definition of doing a true needs analysis, defining and building a concept, and then selling that concept as the solution.

Utiising Insight across the sales cycle

What it does is help to build and package insight into a game plan to support the sales team 'go to market' and bring insight into different areas of the sales cycle to build confidence and credibility that will influence the customers mind.

When reviewing the insight and how to package it accordingly consider what the value of the insight brings:

1. Does this insight teach something to help us pivot or refocus our Distinctive selling points?
2. Does the insight help reinforce our advantages and therefore create benefits?
3. Does the insight help challenge the status quo and lead to our value proposition?
4. Can we package this insight for marketing messages?

Determining the impact of the insight, it can then be tailored and implemented by the team at the right time. Below are some areas where insight can have a strong impact:

Messaging:	Based on the insight, can we use it to extend our marketing and advertising messaging at scale?
Opening Statements:	Utilising this insight, what new opening statements or Initial positioning statements can be crafted to challenge the status quo, including reframing and behaviour change?
Discovery questions:	Understanding the insight, what questions should be asked to lead the customer towards particular DSPs in your product or service?
Demonstrations:	How do you bring the insight into play by storytelling and selling the value proposition
Demonstrable PBOs:	Instead of demonstrating a return on investment, can we craft specific positive business outcomes that are realigned to value proposition and our customer business objectives, showcasing examples from the insight?
Objection Handling:	Does the insight enable objections to be predetermined and therefore addressed early?

Who Crafts the Gameplan

We started at the beginning of the insight factory chapter by asking who is responsible for generating insight and in that chapter, it was agreed that insight comes from a variety of factors. Now the question is, who is responsible for crafting that insight into useable content? My thoughts are that there is only one department that has the skill and resources to do it – Marketing. Marketing has the tools to create organisational-wide, repeatable messaging, and impact all departments. Sales, on the other hand, need to be able to take those messages and bring them to life with individual clients.

Building Sales Agility

Having looked at building the insight factory and packaging insight to get sales engaged with it, let's move on to generating that Agile approach on how to adapt to the insight. Agility is not a buzzword, it's an imperative. The tech industry is characterized by its dynamic and ever-evolving nature especially as new technologies emerge, customer preferences shift, and competitors innovate at breakneck speeds. In such a volatile environment, a rigid approach can quickly render a business obsolete. Agility ensures that businesses can pivot and adapt to these changes, seizing new opportunities and mitigating potential threats.

I have spoken about Sales Agility for many years, having an organisation that you can drop something into the top of the enterprise and it just knows what to do with it, all the cogs work together and success is spat out the other end. Michelle Vazzana and Lisa Sottosanti Doyle, who co-authored "The Sales Agility Code" shares how developing mental agility and decision-making in sales, emphasizing the need for an agile approach due to the unpredictable and competitive nature of modern sales environments. They propose a method that allows salespeople to adapt their approach based on the buying situations they encounter. The ability to respond rapidly to emerging situations can be the difference between seizing an opportunity and watching it slip away. But rapid responsiveness is not about hasty, impulsive reactions; it's about swift, informed, and strategic actions.

Rapid Responsiveness

Before you can respond rapidly, you must be prepared. This means always being on the lookout for new information, whether it's about market trends, customer preferences, or competitor actions. By staying informed, you position yourself to act quickly when the need arises. In the previous chapters we have looked at ways to keep insights at the forefront of both internal sales meetings and creating a more systemised approach to capturing it.

Empowering the team with real-time data is also extremely useful. Back in the day, we used to create the idea of a Taxi Pack. This was a brief about the various pieces of insight we could present as if the person had to read it in the back of a taxi. Think of it like a briefing document for James Bond!

But responsiveness in sales is not just about being fast. Jill Konrath in her book 'Agile Selling' highlights 5 key attributes on driving agility and responsiveness:

Rapid Learning is Crucial:	In the modern sales world, products, services, and tools are continuously evolving. Salespeople must become rapid learners to keep up – consider breaking down information into bite-sized chunks and focusing on the most critical details first.
Agility Over Perfection:	It's more important to be adaptable and responsive than to have a perfect sales pitch or strategy. Being agile allows salespeople to pivot when faced with new challenges or information.
Understand Your Customer:	In an age of information overload, customers value salespeople who can provide clarity and insight. Taking the time to truly understand customer needs and challenges allows for more tailored and effective sales approaches.
Leverage Technology:	Modern sales tools and technologies can significantly enhance agility. Whether it's CRM systems, data analytics, or communication tools, leveraging technology can provide valuable insights and streamline the sales process.
Mindset Matters:	A Growth mindset is characterized by curiosity, resilience, and a willingness to step out of one's comfort zone. Cultivating this mindset is crucial for success in the modern sales world.

As described above mindset matters. Curiosity, resilience and stepping out of the comfort zone are all traits that are tough to teach. However, developing a Growth mindset can happen especially if the culture is designed around continuous improvement and learning from both wins and setbacks.

A Growth Mindset

A growth mindset, a concept pioneered by psychologist Carol Dweck in her ground-breaking work, "Mindset: The New Psychology of Success," is the belief that one's abilities and intelligence can be developed through dedication, hard work, and perseverance. Dweck's research delineates how this mindset not only influences individual achievement but also impacts how teams and organizations approach challenges and learning opportunities. In the context of sales, and as we explore the need for agility and high adaptability, a growth mindset is invaluable. It encourages sales teams and professionals to view setbacks not as insurmountable obstacles but as opportunities for learning and growth.

The importance of a growth mindset in building insight agility cannot be overstated. Insight agility refers to the ability of sales teams to quickly gather, interpret, and act on customer data and market trends. In an environment characterized by rapid change and high competition, the capacity to pivot and adapt strategies based on new insights is crucial. A growth mindset fosters a culture of continuous learning and curiosity, essential for developing insight agility.

Sales teams with a growth mindset are more likely to experiment with new approaches, learn from their outcomes, and refine their strategies—turning insights into actionable intelligence with speed and efficiency. By embracing challenges, persisting in the face of setbacks, and learning from criticism, these teams position themselves not just to respond to market dynamics but to anticipate and shape them, driving innovation and achieving sustainable success.

Skill Augmentation

To build and utilise agility one of the core components is ensuring you augment the teams' skillsets. Skills augmentation refers to the process of enhancing, expanding, or adding to the existing skill set of an individual or a team. It's about identifying gaps or areas of improvement in one's current abilities and then taking deliberate steps to elevate those skills to a higher level. This can be achieved through various means such as training, workshops, mentoring, or even hands-on experience.

Consider both technical skills in terms of product, but also ongoing training and development in areas like industry knowledge, market knowledge, and of course sales skills and capability.

As the market also adapts, changes and evolves, the ability to engage with customers on an emotional level will be paramount. I know these are often referred to as soft skills, but they are hard to develop. Consider aspects of empathy, communication and relationship building which are crucial when selling in a tougher climate. More about this in Force 5 – Emotional Intelligence!

Market Knowledge

Create regular training, education and learning sessions to keep the team abreast of the changes and advancements in the market and industry. Invite people from strategy, marketing, account managers, product etc, to share what is going on.

These sessions do not need to be long, but it does need to keep them up to date with those constant changes.

Cross Training

Encourage sales team members to learn about areas adjacent to their primary role. This could be understanding the technical aspects of the product, diving into customer success strategies, or even understanding the financial side of the business. This holistic understanding can lead to better sales strategies and customer interactions. Cross-training allows salespeople to gain insights into various facets of the business, from product development to customer support. This comprehensive understanding enables them to address customer queries more effectively, anticipate potential objections, and position the product or service in a way that resonates with the customer's specific needs.

Edward Lawler and Chris Worley's work on building adaptable organizations often touches upon the need for employees to have a broad understanding of various parts of the business. Their insights can be applied to the benefits of cross-training in fostering an agile and resilient workforce, which is exactly what we need to build.

Markets are dynamic, and customer needs evolve. A cross-trained salesperson can quickly adapt to changing circumstances, whether it's a shift in market trends, a new product launch, or a fast change in company strategy. Their diverse skill set allows them to pivot and adjust their sales approach accordingly.

When salespeople have a grasp of what other departments do, it fosters better inter-departmental collaboration. They can liaise more effectively with marketing, product development, or customer support teams, ensuring a seamless flow of information and a unified approach to customer engagement.

Cross-training reduces dependency and increases agility.
In her book "Multipliers: How the Best Leaders Make Everyone Smarter," Liz Wiseman explores how leaders can unlock the potential of their teams by cross-training and maximizing their team capabilities, thus fostering an environment where learning across different domains is encouraged. It never ceases to amaze how many large organisations still struggle to even get their leadership team to cross-train as well. People can make it to the top of their vertical, even as an MD or Head of Sales, they have high-spending clients, generating sizeable revenue, but they can't cross-sell the organisation's other products or services/service lines.

Cross training from an organisational perspective allows you to pivot your resources where necessary. If one particular segment or target market is floundering, you can reassign some of your resources to other areas. If a key salesperson/account manager is unavailable, others with similar training can step in, ensuring that sales operations continue without disruption. This is especially crucial for SaaS and Tech businesses where rapid response times can be a competitive advantage.

Knowledge Sharing and Feedback Loops

We saw back in the chapter on building an 'Insight Factory' aspects of knowledge sharing and capturing insight. Building a Growth Mindset in the team is about creating a learning culture where people are looking and willing to grow. Look for ways to engage the team to share experiences and knowledge. Consider aspects like Team meetings, call levelling and listening to live sales calls.

Team Meetings

One of the things I have experienced and found valuable is to book a learning aspect to every team meeting. This can come in a number of formats:

Kick off with a 'Teach'. Every team meeting, or morning huddle, try to have one of the team members deliver short session to teach the team something new. This works well as a rotation, someone new each meeting, and put a short time limit on it, 5 mins for example. Doing this relieves any pressure on the setup and structure of the teaching point. Empowering the individual to pick the topic and the 'teach' will help build the learning culture. Also allow the 'teach' to not always be work-related, this way you can have a wider engagement and bring more fun and laughter to the meeting.

Special Guests – Invite different departments to come along to the team meetings to share knowledge and deliver insight to the team. Make the special guests get involved in the meeting, not just turn up and deliver some PowerPoint slides and disappear again. If Marketing, Product team, Strategy, Customer Success or other team members come along, they have a different view of some of the opportunities and threats, and can also provide different perspectives on the world to the team. Equally, sharing information will enable a shift in strategic direction or sales approach.

Deal Reviews – In the team meeting have the team share some of the wins and challenges in the group. Share some of the key learnings and open the conversation up to the group for group engagement. Be particular in capturing the good insight, and exploring the challenges openly.

Double Loop Learning – in the previous chapters we looked at Double Loop Learning and Feedback. Remember where a single loop looks at the problem and looks at actions to resolve it, double-loop Learning goes a step further. Instead of just adjusting actions, it questions the underlying assumptions and beliefs that lead to those actions. Utilise double loop learning to have the team try go deeper into the cause and effect. It is the 'Peel the Onion' effect to try and ascertain the cause of the cause. i.e. what is cause the is creating the problem.

Call Leveling

Call levelling is a great exercise to do if you have the opportunity to listen to calls. Call Levelling, often referred to as "Call Review" or "Call Coaching," is a collaborative exercise where sales team members, together with their managers or peers, review and analyse recorded sales calls. The objective is to identify areas of strength, uncover opportunities for improvement, and share best practices. It provides a wealth of information about customer needs, objections, and decision-making processes. By regularly reviewing these calls, you can gain insights into your communication style, understand customer challenges better, and refine your pitch. It's a real-time feedback mechanism that's invaluable for personal development.

Team meetings are an excellent platform for Call Levelling. Not only does it allow for collective feedback, but it also promotes a culture of transparency and shared learning. By discussing specific calls in a group setting, you can benefit from diverse perspectives, leading to richer insights and more comprehensive feedback. It also ensures that best practices and valuable learnings are disseminated across the team, elevating everyone's performance. It also gets past the 'what are they doing differently from me to get the better results'.

Some quick guiding points for these sessions:

Regular Review	Make this a regular aspect of continuous learning and ensure it happens each week or month.
Ask people to nominate calls	There is little point using call levelling on poor calls so ask people to nominate a couple of their best calls this week/month. Ensure you utilise different people, not always the top performers.
Constructive Feedback	The goal isn't to criticize but to improve. Celebrate the wins and view areas of improvement as opportunities for growth.
Group Discussion	Have the group share 1: what went well and then 2: what could have made it better. This means everything is kept positive and not focused on what didn't go so well! Ask the group if they had any learning points themselves from the call.

Incorporating Call Levelling into your continuous learning journey ensures that you're not just learning in theory but are also refining your practice. It's a hands-on approach to development that yields tangible results, making you more attuned to your customers and more effective in your sales efforts.

Call Listening & Accompaniments

Taking the call levelling to another level is to have the senior team members attend sales calls or listen to some of the sales recordings and provide coaching and feedback. The senior team often think differently and see the business from different angles. Having them provide coaching and feedback to the sales team provides them a diverse viewpoint and again will increase their learning and development. This collective intelligence can be a significant advantage in navigating market changes, challenges, and opportunities.

4 Areas of High-Performing Agility

When looking to build continuous learning and development, and also a Learning Culture, you need to assess behaviour, not just knowledge. Knowing What to do and Being Able to Do It are two very different things. And then even if they know what to do, and are capable of doing it, are they actually doing it?

There are four areas to consider when building agility and driving a high-performance culture:

Do our people:

1: Know what to do	- do our people know what to do, is it clear, are the educated
2: Able to do it	- are they able to do it, do they have the skill and capability
3: Equipped to do it	- do they have the tools, resources and resourcefulness to do it
4: Want to do it	- are they motivated, do they have the desire to make it happen

When looking at your organisation, consider these four areas and determine what areas you currently perform well in, and perhaps where you may have a shortfall.

Know what to do

Knowing what to do is a strong concept and not to be underestimated. Challenge yourself and the management team to ensure people know what to do. Look at each of the sales stages, the activities within it and the knowledge skill and behaviours expected within it. Firstly assess whether the management team and coaches truly understand the tools and techniques. These people will be responsible for making it happen and if they are not familiar with the new ways of working, don't expect the behaviour to be reinforced. Testing knowledge is one of the easiest aspects of assessment. Utilise quizzes, daily challenges, or online tools to deliver training and or test their retention.

Able to do it

People might know what to do, but can they do it. For example, you may know how a bike works, there are 2 wheels, a chain attached to some pedals, and when you cycle the pedals around it rotates the back wheel and propels you forward. This doesn't mean that you can ride the bike! The same rules apply to sales. You may know that you need to ask questions, you may even know the question types to ask – that doesn't mean that you can use them in earnest.

To evaluate an individual's capabilities, utilsiing role plays and observing sales are commonly used. I use the term real play instead of role play as we should make the event as real as possible. When assessing, and driving behaviour change, consider how to assist the salesperson spot what is going well and what they have missed. Opposite is an extract of a sales observation form used with some of our clients. This is a great tool to help people spot areas that they excel in, and areas they potentially could do better.

Concentrating on behaviour and providing coaching goes beyond mere checklist items like "did you do this or that". Instead, this observation sheet focuses on what went well in the sales call and what could be improved. The example opposite looks at 10 behaviours within a sales call, five behaviours for connecting with customers and five behaviours for Exploring customers' wants and needs. The focus here isn't a checklist to determine whether they did it or not, it is about how well they did it. The scoring system in this example is 1 to 5 where 1 is well below expectation, 5 is Exceptional, a 3 is met expectations. This provides the coach and coachee something to work on.

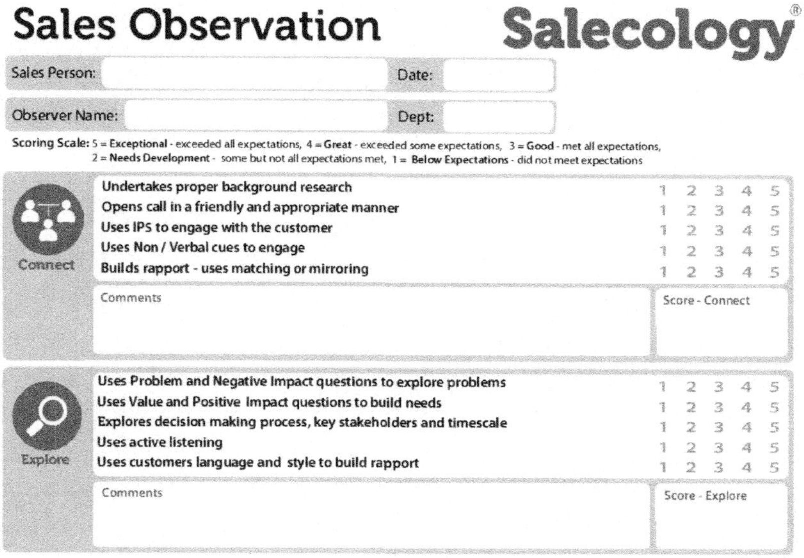

Sales Observation

Salecology®

Sales Person:	Date:
Observer Name:	Dept:

Scoring Scale: 5 = **Exceptional** - exceeded all expectations, 4 = **Great** - exceeded some expectations, 3 = **Good** - met all expectations, 2 = **Needs Development** - some but not all expectations met, 1 = **Below Expectations** - did not meet expectations

Connect		
	Undertakes proper background research	1 2 3 4 5
	Opens call in a friendly and appropriate manner	1 2 3 4 5
	Uses IPS to engage with the customer	1 2 3 4 5
	Uses Non / Verbal cues to engage	1 2 3 4 5
	Builds rapport - uses matching or mirroring	1 2 3 4 5
	Comments	Score - Connect

Explore		
	Uses Problem and Negative Impact questions to explore problems	1 2 3 4 5
	Uses Value and Positive Impact questions to build needs	1 2 3 4 5
	Explores decision making process, key stakeholders and timescale	1 2 3 4 5
	Uses active listening	1 2 3 4 5
	Uses customers language and style to build rapport	1 2 3 4 5
	Comments	Score - Explore

Using observation forms, coupled with effective coaching and feedback, helps distinguish between knowing what to do and executing it. Recording the sales call and reviewing it together, with both parties filling out the form, facilitates focused discussions on growth. Review the scores and select one or two areas to improve upon for the next call.

Equipped to do it

This aspect asks the question of whether people have the tools and resources necessary to undertake the work. You might know what to do, even able to do it, but just don't have the equipment to do it.

We have reviewed previously the insight factory, and packaging insight for the sales team, but also consider all other aspects to determine whether people have the right tools for the job. To build agility into the team there is a mix of having the resources and being resourceful. The team need to know how to marshal resources and find things they need, but for the organisation to provide a competitive advantage they should also ensure they have as much as can be provided.

Interestingly, many organisations provide so many resources that the team either doesn't use them or worse still doesn't know how to use them. Consider assessing and testing the team's ability to use the resources at their disposal and also run development sessions on how to be resourceful.

Want to do it

The 3 items above could all be implemented skilfully but if those people you are working with are not mentally and physically engaged, i.e. if they don't want to do it then the first 3 are redundant. We need to identify if people are motivated to do things.

Motivations are the things that drive people to do the things they do. It is underpinned by personal values, but also our natural tendencies to move toward or away from things. When assessing people's motivations, especially within the sales roles and organisation, you need to consider intrinsic and extrinsic motivations. I believe it was Edward Deci and Richard Ryan in their book on Self-Determination Theory (SDT), which introduced us to a framework for understanding human motivation and personality, where they determined intrinsic motivation, which arises from internal rewards and personal satisfaction, and extrinsic motivation, which involves external rewards or pressures.

Intrinsic motivations	activities people find enjoyable and derive personal satisfaction from
Extrinsic motivations	driven by external factors such as monetary reward.

The intrinsic motivations are by far more compelling and will be used as the person's morale compass, but also determine which parts of the role they will tend to gravitate towards and which ones to shy away from.

Extrinsic motivations evolve as time progresses. Whilst most often think that sales people are driven by money and commission it is not always the case. It's tempting to delve into Maslow's hierarchy of needs, but I think it is easier to say that yes it's evident that those in the early stages of their careers are commonly driven by financial rewards. However, as they attain more success, other factors tend to take precedence.

Distinct variations in motivations are also evident across generations such as Baby Boomers, Gen X, Millennials, and Gen Z. For instance, Gen Z individuals seem to prioritize organizations offering robust growth prospects and an entrepreneurial spirit. In contrast, Millennials appeared more attracted to workplace perks, like fun office environments with ping pong tables or pet-friendly policies such as 'bring your dog to work'.

Understanding what motivations and values the person has, will enable you to determine whether they can succeed, enjoy and flourish in the environment they will be working in, and also provide intelligence to build better reward and recognition systems to drive their performance, even when the going is tough.

Is it a Skill or a Will Issue

The second part of developing your agile sales team and enabling a growth mindset is to identify what is holding the individual or team back. Is it that they know what to do but are unable to do it (skill) or is it that they know what they should be doing but they just don't do it (Will).

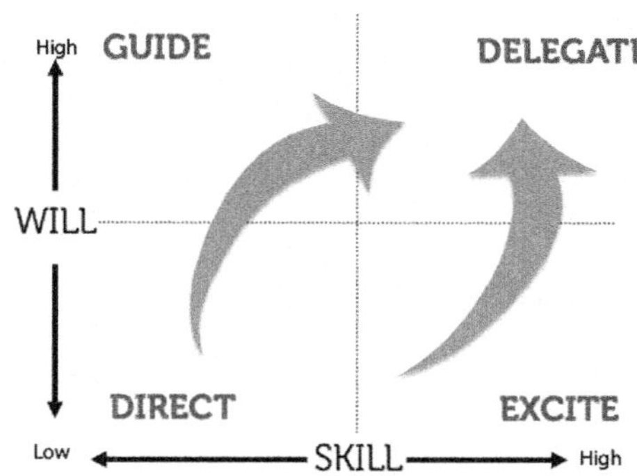

Too often the sales manager/ coach reaches for the training button to educate the individual when it is not really a skill issue at all, it is more of a motivational issue. Take a sales person who has been successful to date, believes they know it all, and although things are changing and they need to adapt their style and approach, they are resistant to do so. From an insight perspective, flooding them with more data, more insight, more intelligence, won't make any difference. Max Landsberg, in his book the Tao of Coaching, modelled different behaviours to utilise depending on where people sat on the Skill / Will matrix.

High Will, Low Skill

When individuals first start in a new role or assume fresh duties, it's typical to encounter those with a heightened eagerness and receptiveness to innovative concepts and a willingness to adopt new skills and practices. Collaborating with such enthusiastic individuals can be rewarding as they ardently pursue success. In such cases, the coaching approach falls under the title "Guidance." This coaching style leans heavily into training and instructing, catering to a genuinely receptive individual. It's crucial to offer clear directions, schedule regular weekly touchpoints, and contemplate ways to commend their efforts and uplift their morale. Acknowledge that they might make mistakes occasionally, but viewing those as learning opportunities is vital to their growth.

High Will, High Skill

These are your high performers; they have above-average skills and capabilities to deliver the tasks and the motivation to make it happen. These individuals stand out as top-tier contributors, possessing both the adeptness for tasks and the zeal to execute them. While you may find yourself gravitating towards this group due to the enriching experience and learning they offer, it's essential to continually support them. This ensures they sustain their energy and passion, avoiding any decline in their motivation.

From a mentoring standpoint, the focus should shift towards empowering them. This lets them fully embrace and apply new behaviours while also engaging in dialogues about their personal growth aspirations. Because of their high will and high skill, these people also tend to look for any new nugget of information that they can add to their repertoire that will enable them to increase performance.

High Skill, Low Will

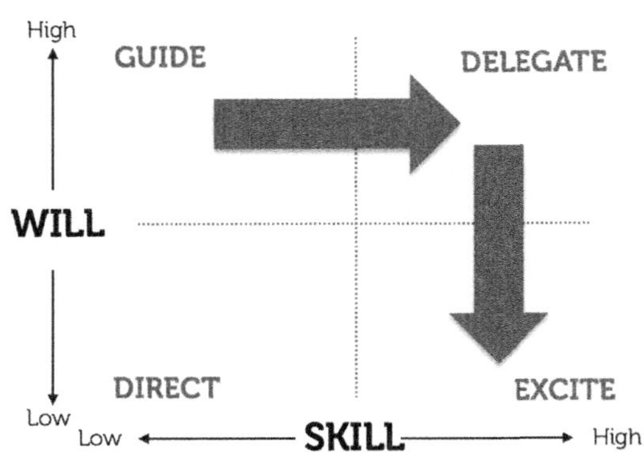

Sadly, the direction of travel for many people in a workplace can be from High Will /Low Skill to High Skill / High Will, and then they slowly become demotivated and drop to High Skill / Low Will. They sort of start jogging along rather than running like they did before. During an economic downturn, and when market conditions get tougher, you can see this happen as people become a little despondent as well.

This comes down to the person's engagement and the coach / manager's ability to understand why this is happening. It could be that they are no longer being challenged enough or have just got bored with the role and need some new goals or incentives. The role of the coach here is to excite and motivate the person back into the High Will box.

Consider some of the things below:

Job Enlargement –	also known as horizontal expansion, is about increasing the size of the activities of their role i.e bigger area, more product lines, etc,
Job Enrichment -	also known as vertical expansion, is about giving them more opportunities to do different things, I.e. coach others, host some of the sales meetings, mentoring etc
Job Rotation -	move them into a different department or role for a short period to change their work and focus
Projects -	Consider putting them into some special projects to excite them back into the work.

As the coach, the important things to do here is to talk openly with the person to uncover what is driving their demotivation. Then digging deeper, you will be able to see what is possible to excite them back into the high will, high skill mindset.

Low Will, low Skill

In prosperous times marked by rapid expansion and a favourable market, individuals might achieve their sales targets with minimal effort. It's surprising to me how many times I have heard sales representatives frequently mention how "the product really just sells itself". However, when challenges arise, many in this group often don't possess the tenacity or adaptability to intensify their efforts.

Additionally, newcomers still acclimating may fall into this Low Will / Low Skill category if they're hesitant to seek assistance. Greater guidance, education, and backing are imperative for these individuals, particularly if they've just joined the team. Coaches should communicate candidly, outlining expectations, and demonstrating procedures, and if individuals can't adapt or evolve their perspective, it may be time to let them go.

Tailoring your learning is essential for developing sales agility and resilience and becomes undeniably clear that the cornerstone of enduring success lies within the cultivation of a growth mindset. The relentless pursuit of learning is a pivotal role of resilience in the face of adversity, especially when looking to dominate within any economic condition. These elements are not just strategies but fundamental principles that guide the continuous improvement and development of individuals and teams.

By fostering an environment that celebrates curiosity, encourages risk-taking, and views failure as a springboard for growth, organizations can unlock the full potential of their people. In doing so, they not only enhance their capacity to adapt and thrive in an ever-evolving sales landscape but also pave the way for sustainable growth and innovation. As we conclude this chapter, let us carry forward the understanding that developing a growth mindset is essential for driving sales agility and is one that requires persistence, dedication, and a commitment to cultivating the seeds of potential within every individual.

Conclusion

The ability to swiftly adapt, anticipate, and innovate is not just a competitive advantage—it's a necessity. As we've looked at various facets of Insight Agility, it's evident that this isn't a mere strategy, it's a mindset, a culture, and a commitment.

Proactive Problem Solving

Having looked at packing insight, creating a growth mindset and building the level of continuous learning, in essence the key to sustained success and market leadership lies in proactive problem-solving across the organisation. This approach not only prepares you for the challenges ahead but often turns potential obstacles into opportunities.

Anticipating Challenges

Anticipation is definitely something that is needed. Keeping a keen eye on market trends, technological advancements, and shifts in customer preferences, one can often predict challenges before they manifest. Regularly engaging with customers, attending industry conferences, and staying updated with market research are essential practices. Okay, let's not teach you to suck eggs here, for me it is about being purposeful about taking the time to look and listen for signals, not just looking and listening for awareness. This foresight allows you to prepare in advance, ensuring that when a challenge does arise, you're not caught off guard but are ready with a solution.

For instance, if you foresee a regulatory change that might affect how data is handled in your industry, instead of waiting for the regulation to come into effect, you could start adapting your product, service in advance or at least the messaging in advance. This not only ensures compliance but can also be a unique selling point, showcasing your commitment to data security and regulatory adherence.

One of the richest sources of insights is your existing customer base. Regularly engaging with them can provide early warnings about potential challenges. Whether it's feedback about a feature they wish your product had or concerns about upcoming industry regulations, these interactions are goldmines of information. Remember the concept of 'Call Levelling' we discussed earlier? This practice can be instrumental here. By regularly reviewing calls and meetings, salespeople can pick up on subtle hints or recurring themes that might indicate potential challenges on the horizon, not just the objection handling.

Seeking Innovative Solutions

Anticipating challenges is just one part of the equation. The next step is crafting innovative solutions to address these challenges. This requires a mindset that views challenges not as barriers but as puzzles waiting to be solved. Encourage your team to think outside the box, to question the status quo, and to brainstorm collectively. Often, the most innovative solutions arise from collaborative thinking, where diverse perspectives come together.

Consider setting up regular "innovation labs" or brainstorming sessions within your team. Here, challenges can be laid out, and team members can collaboratively ideate on potential solutions. This not only fosters a culture of innovation but also ensures that when a challenge arises, you have a repository of potential solutions to draw from.

Moreover, don't shy away from leveraging technology. The SaaS world is brimming with tools and platforms that can aid in problem-solving. Whether it's data analytics tools that offer insights into customer behaviour or AI-driven platforms that can predict market trends, technology can be a significant ally in your proactive problem-solving journey.

Encourage the sales team to apply their insights in real-world scenarios. Whether it's tailoring a sales pitch based on customer behaviour data or adjusting a sales strategy based on market trends, the true value of the Insight Factory is realized when insights are translated into action.

The Power of Curiosity

At the heart of innovation lies curiosity. Salespeople should cultivate a genuine interest in understanding the intricacies of their product, the nuances of their industry, and the unique challenges their clients face. By asking questions and diving deeper, they can uncover opportunities to offer solutions that might not be immediately apparent. Remember the emphasis we placed on 'Challenging the Status Quo' earlier in the book? This is where it comes into play. By questioning existing processes and solutions, salespeople can identify areas ripe for innovation. I have always found that curiosity is by far one of the most important traits in a sales person. If you are curious and willing to investigate and learn more about it, you are already one step ahead of the bulk of the competition.

Collaboration Breeds Innovation

Innovation is, however, often a collective effort. Salespeople should actively collaborate with different departments within their organisation, from product development to customer support. I have just spoken about the concept of innovation labs, however, collaborating with different departments, e.g by sharing insights from the field and understanding the capabilities and limitations of their product, salespeople can work with their teams to craft bespoke solutions for their clients. This collaborative approach not only leads to more innovative solutions but also positions the salesperson as a bridge between the client and the company, reinforcing trust.

Continuous Learning is Key

Innovation and learning go hand in hand. Salespeople should invest time in upskilling, attending workshops, and participating in industry conferences. By staying updated with the latest trends and best practices, they can bring fresh perspectives and ideas to the table. Our earlier discussions on Growth Mindset highlighted the importance of this aspect, and it's worth reiterating here.

By embracing an Insight-Infused Strategy, sales organizations can navigate the complex sales landscape with unmatched precision and foresight. It's about turning insights into action, data into decisions, and feedback into formidable strategies.

Final thought

From harnessing the power of data to inform decisions to fostering a culture of continuous learning, the principles of Insight Agility are deeply rooted in proactivity. It's about not just reacting to the market's ebbs and flows but shaping them, leading the charge, and setting the pace. By challenging the status quo, salespeople can redefine what's possible, pushing boundaries and consistently delivering value to their clients.

The emphasis on proactive problem-solving underscores the importance of not just addressing challenges but anticipating them. In a market where change is the only constant, the ability to foresee potential hurdles and navigate them with finesse can set a salesperson apart.

Moreover, the pursuit of innovative solutions serves as a testament to the limitless potential of the industry. With the continual advancement of technology, there is always a new frontier to explore, a novel solution to craft, and a unique value proposition to offer.

However, at the heart of Insight Agility is the individual—the salesperson. Their curiosity, dedication, and drive to continuously upskill and adapt are what breathe life into these principles. It's their on-ground insights, their interactions with clients, and their relentless pursuit of excellence that transform these strategies into tangible results.

3

Force 3:
Client Centricity

Contents

Client Centricity

Our journey began in this book with Force 1, where we embraced a Disruptive Mindset, challenging traditional norms and constantly seeking avenues for innovation. In Force 2, we honed our Insight Agility, leveraging data-driven insights to anticipate market shifts and foster a culture of continuous learning. These foundational forces pave the way for a third and pivotal force: Client Centricity.

We have already discussed that items such as features and functionalities can quickly be replicated. Therefore, a true differentiator lies in the depth and quality of relationships a business nurtures with its clients. Client Centricity is often banded around, but it is a great compass that directs every decision, strategy, and interaction in a business. But what does it truly mean to be client-centric, especially in the face of an economic downturn?

Ever since the internet took off in the early noughties people have been taught to 'Go Compare', so much so that there is now a strong belief that that whatever one company is selling you can probably go online and find it somewhere else and probably cheaper. Therefore what differentiates one company over another is not just the product or solution but a valued trusted partner who can visualise and articulate the value they bring, adapt offers to the customers evolving needs, and guide them towards achieving tangible outcomes. This is the essence of Client Centricity.

Delivering Undeniable Value at Every Touchpoint

As much as this is a given in the good times, in challenging economic times, clients are more discerning about where they invest their resources. Now, more than ever, businesses need to move beyond superficial interactions and cultivate deep, meaningful relationships. This means truly understanding clients' evolving challenges, anticipating their needs, and being a consistent source of value and support.

Every interaction, whether it's a product demo, a support ticket resolution, or a quarterly review, is an opportunity to reinforce value. Client Centricity is about ensuring that at every touchpoint, clients are reminded of why they chose your organisation and solution in the first place. It's about demonstrating not just the value of the technology, but the value of the partnership.

A key component of this is the concept of 'Customer Success', especially crucial in software solutions. It's not just about making a sale, it's about:

- **Time to Live** - Quickly integrate the solution into their operations
- **Time to Value** - Helping them realise the benefits you sold them
- **Time to Grow**- Having seen the above two, uncovering new opportunities

This journey, from onboarding to expansion, underscores the importance of building and nurturing long-term relationships.

Economic climate change also brings unique challenges for clients. Budgets are tighter, needs change, and uncertainty is abound. A client-centric business proactively addresses these challenges, offering flexible solutions, tailored packages and even strategic consultations to help clients navigate these turbulent waters.

Client Centricity involves proactive engagement not waiting for customers to reach out. It means regularly checking in, seeking feedback and offering insights or recommendations even before the client realizes they need them. It's about being one step ahead, solidifying your position as a trusted partner.

Through this Force / part of the book, we'll delve deeper into each of these facets, exploring the nuances of Client Centricity in the world of tech and software solutions, especially in the context of a slower economy. That said, these things are important in both good as well as in turbulent times.

Putting the customer at the heart of what we do?

Client Centricity is a strategic approach where the client's needs, preferences, and expectations are placed at the core of a company's decision-making processes, operations, and culture. It goes beyond mere customer service, encompassing every touchpoint and interaction a client has with a business. A client-centric organisation prioritises building and nurturing long-term relationships, ensuring that solutions, products, and services are tailored to meet the unique requirements and aspirations of its clients. By adopting a client-centric mindset, businesses aim to enhance client satisfaction, loyalty, and advocacy, ultimately driving sustainable growth and competitive advantage.

According to the following people it evolves into:

Jeff Bezos, founder of Amazon	"We see our customers as invited guests to a party, and we are the hosts. It's our job every day to make every important aspect of the customer experience a little bit better."
Philip Kotler, marketing professor	"The most important thing is to forecast where customers are moving, and be in front of them."
Peter Fader, author	"Customer centricity is a strategy to fundamentally align a company's products and services with the wants and needs of its most valuable customers."

So, it is quite a mixed bag when we talk about being client-centric. The key is to review each touchpoint the organisation has with the client and build the right level of engagement and experience to ensure that the customer sees value and feels valued.

The Customer Journey

It all begins with the customer journey where Sales and Marketing come together. Taking time out to consider how the customer goes though their buying process will enable you to spot the various touch points you have with them and maximise your opportunity to continue to build trust at each point.

Mapping the Journey

The customer journey can be mapped to quite a deep level and look at the touch points which start long before the customer engages with a sales person, and quite often long before they even start shopping around for products. Digital marketeers will be quick to tell you that there are passive moment where the customer subconsciously notices things, either through marketing activity or that the customer is simply becoming frustrated as things are changing in their world and they are starting to become conscious that they might need to do something about it.

On the B2B (business-to-business) front, according to the statistics from Saleslion in 2023, approximately 77% of B2B buyers reported that they would not even speak to a salesperson until they had conducted their own research. This statistic highlights the critical need for businesses to ensure that comprehensive, informative, and easily accessible content is available to potential clients, aiming to support their research process and influence their purchasing decisions positively.

Additionally, content marketing plays a pivotal role in engaging potential customers, with 44% of consumers typically consuming three to five pieces of content before engaging with a vendor. This indicates a clear preference for engaging with informative and valuable content as part of the research process before initiating contact with sales teams. These findings emphasize the importance for businesses to adapt their strategies towards providing valuable information and fostering a strong online presence.

By understanding and catering to the research habits of their potential customers, businesses can better position themselves in a competitive market, ensuring they meet the evolving expectations of both individual consumers and business clients.

The first step in mapping the journey is to consider:

1: What are they doing
2: Where are they doing it
3: What do they want and need

Also as you start thinking about these 3 steps, you also should make this **more emotionally intelligent** and add 2 more pieces to this journey:

4: What are they thinking
5: How are they feeling

This reflection provides huge empathy with the customer throughout their journey and provides insight into how to differentiate the touch points, build rapport and influence the outcome. I often find working through the "how are they feeling" part of the customer journey the most enlightening.

Understanding this emotional aspect of the customer journey helps the seller manage the customer in a much better way, demonstrating empathy, but also becoming proactive in minimising the fluctuations of emotions. Also by understanding the emotions, enables you to build better sales tools to continue to build confidence in selecting the seller and the organisation throughout the process.

Mapping the Sales Cycle

Having defined the customer journey, it becomes easier to wrap the sales process around it. Consider each step the customer goes through and align it to the various stages for your sales process.

A lot of organisations utilise the default pipeline names provided from their CRM system. Although useful and better than nothing, consider creating your own that are more meaningful for the sales process and customer journey.

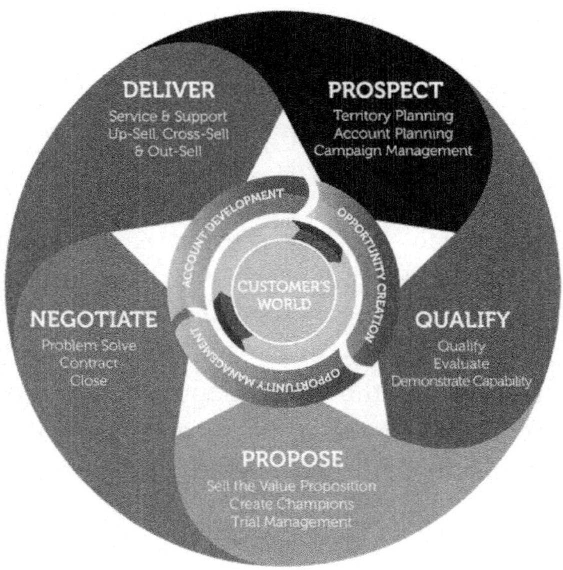

The image above, demonstrates a typical sales cycle that is wrapped around the customer journey / buying cycle.

Example Process

Below is an example of how that was mapped.

Prospect – mapping the territory, the accounts within it and building out the sales campaigns.

Qualify – this covers perhaps a couple of key steps, qualify whether an opportunity exists, and evaluate whether it is worth pursuing.

For SaaS type organisations the Qualify stage often includes demonstrating capability and credibility. Like the experience of SalesForce.com, as mapped in the book Predictable Revenue by Aaron Ross, the Prospecting and Qualify stage may be owned by a sales development representative (SDR) who warms up opportunities and then hands them across to an Account Executive (AE) who will take it the rest of the way through the sales cycle. The Demonstrate capability/credibility would only encompass a small demo of the product, if at all. Usually, it is demonstrating how the solution would help meet the needs, not an actual product demonstration.

Propose – This stage is where the seller, moves into demonstrating the value of the solution and moving into formal needs and how it matches the customer's criteria. From a Salecology EQ perspective, the seller should also move from selling to their champion to selling with them into the rest of the organisation.

Negotiate – This part of the sales cycle is about problem solving, objection handling as well as negotiating the close. It covers off those steps of getting the terms and conditions aligned and getting the deal signed off.

Deliver – is therefore about ensuring the customer is satisfied that the solution delivers on their needs and then moves into selling additional products and services before the contract renewal takes place.

For many organisations, once the customer has signed, the account is handed over to the Customer Success (CS) team who are focused on getting the customer live on the system and managing the relationship afterwards, including renewals, up sells and potentially cross-selling.

Charting out the customer journey alongside the sales process allows the organisation to refine its strategies, tools, and resources, fostering a customer-centric sales approach. These principles should be implemented throughout the entire sales cycle, whether engaging with new prospects or nurturing existing accounts.

Deep Dive Engagement

Within the realm of Client Centricity, one of the most pivotal elements is the concept of 'Deep Dive Engagement'. This is a commitment to truly understanding and immersing oneself in the client's world which is a competitive landscape where products and services often overlap in features and benefits, the depth of engagement can be the distinguishing factor that sets one provider apart from another. Deep Dive Engagement is about transcending transactional interactions and fostering meaningful connections. It's about not just hearing but actively listening to the client's needs, challenges, and aspirations. It's about collaborative exploration, where the sales team and the client co-create solutions, ensuring that the client feels deeply involved, valued, and understood.

In software and technological solutions, the benefits of a product are often multifaceted, encompassing both tangible and intangible aspects. While the tangible benefits might be evident in features and functionalities and measured ROI's, the intangible benefits, such as trust, reliability, and partnership, are often realized through a deeper engagement. It's the bridge that connects clients to solutions, making them feel seen and heard. It's the process of not just offering a product but crafting and delivering a tailored solution that resonates with the client's unique challenges and goals.

The Customer's Voice

Listening to your customers is more than just hearing words, it's about truly understanding the essence behind them. It's the art of being fully present, giving undivided attention, and making the speaker feel genuinely heard and valued.

Active Listening in the context of sales, especially in the tech space, is not just a communication technique; it's a strategic approach. Here's why:

Unearthing Hidden Needs:	Clients often come with a set of requirements, but beneath the surface, there might be underlying challenges or aspirations they haven't articulated. Active listening allows sales professionals to pick up on subtle cues, ask probing questions, and uncover these hidden needs.
Building Trust:	When clients feel truly listened to, it fosters a sense of trust. They recognise that they're not just another lead or prospect but a valued partner. This trust is the foundation for a long-lasting relationship, essential in the subscription-based SaaS model.
Tailoring Solutions:	With a deep understanding of the client's needs, sales teams can tailor their solutions more effectively. It's not about pushing a one-size-fits-all product but about crafting a solution that aligns perfectly with the client's unique challenges and goals.
Avoiding Misunderstandings:	Active listening minimises the chances of miscommunication. By clarifying and confirming understanding at every step, sales teams can ensure that both parties are on the same page, reducing the potential for future conflicts or dissatisfaction.
Empowering Clients:	When clients are actively listened to, they feel empowered. They become more open to sharing their concerns, feedback, and ideas, leading to a more collaborative and co-creative sales process.

Incorporating active listening into the sales process might require a shift in mindset for some sales professionals. It's about moving away from the urge to 'sell' and instead focusing on 'serving' the client. It's about pausing, asking open-ended questions, and resisting the temptation to jump in with solutions immediately. It's about valuing the pauses and the silences and using them as opportunities to reflect and understand deeper. This goes back to some of the traits we mentioned in previous chapters, the salesperson needs to be curious.

The challenge in the sales organisation is that you tend to see some other types of listening which are disguised as active such as Assumptive Listening and Attentive Listening.

Are you listening?

Assumptive Listening

Potentially the most annoying type of listening, and one that salespeople can fall into the trap of is that of Assumptive Listening. In fact Assumptive listening is almost an oxymoron, the person might ask a question and already assume they know the answer. Those assumptive listeners have a bad tendency to cut people off before they answer with phrases like "I know what you're going to say" or, somehow even worse, answering the question for them.

Assumptive listeners also might pose a question but, instead of genuinely listening to the response, they're merely biding time until they can speak again, i.e. waiting to talk. It's as if they're eagerly waiting for a cue to dive into their bag and showcase their brochure.

Attentive Listening

Attentive listening isn't a bad thing, you have a person who is listening to the other person. They are paying close attention to what is being said and demonstrate that to the other person by potentially noting down some of the points and capturing the data, maintain some eye contact, their body language provides confirmations like nodding their head at regular intervals, and they are responding with some verbal affirmations such as ah ha, ok, right, yes.

Attentive also means that they listen and respond with follow-up questions, and ensure the person feels like they are being listened to as they are engaged in what they have to say. Although good, active listening can miss out on building deeper more meaningful connections.

Active Listening

For a lot of people, the 'Attentive' listening above was what they had been taught as 'Active Listening', i.e., listen and respond. Active listening takes a lot more work as rather than listening to what the customer is saying, the focus of being Active is to ensure you are listening to the story and trying to ascertain *why the story is the story* so we can get a deeper more meaningful conversation, and potentially spot the emotional triggers in the customer.

Uncovering the story

John Medina stated our brain runs on 12 watts of power and uses about 20% of the bodies energy when it is in a rest state. Therefore, it is designed to run as efficiently as possible, almost in tick-over, and will not fire up the brain unless it is necessary. Therefore to truly get to understand your customer, and actively listen, you need to wait for the system to fire up, and then listen for the emotional aspects, as well as the thoughts of the customer.

Level 1 – Fast Logic

When the person you are talking to first starts to speak on a topic, they will give you information and data straight from the top of their head. The pieces of data held in short-term memory. This fast logic is interesting and will give you some background to the story and some form of context, but it doesn't provide many clues about the person, what they think or feel about the situation.

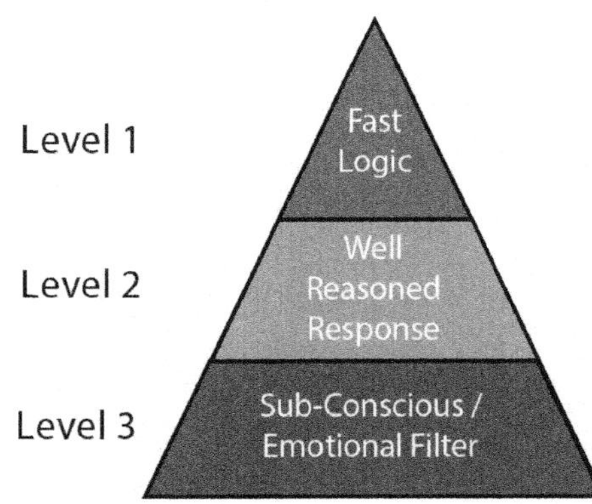

In psychology this is sometimes referred to as noise as it can get in the way of understanding the real part of the story. Imagine you ask someone a simple question, 'how are you?' Quite often the response will be 'fine thanks'. It is an instant response, and the computer doesn't want to fire up the processor and hard disk for this response. Even in a sales context, when you ask someone what they are looking for, they will provide you with some fast logic and tell you some top line functionality or requirements.

Level 2 – Well reasoned response

Once the person has shared with you the fast logic, and noticed that you are still interested and wanting more, the brain will need to fire up and add some processing power to the information, and potentially grab some more data from the memory banks. You will notice a change in the story at this point as the person either changes direction, moves to a different stance, or adds more colour to the story. Here you will get a lot more information, not only will you get a deeper context to the story but you may also get more subtext about the persons thinking and the meaning behind it.

The challenge with trying to actively listen is that as the person shares information with you, your brain has a tendency to make some decisions or judgements based on the data. It looks for linkages and previous experiences you may have encountered, and it applies judgement against the information, almost like an inner voice. To get to level 3, you will need to turn this off.

Level 3 – Why the story is the story

The third level when listening is to understand why the story is the story. The person won't say this, but you will be able to use your intuition, and questions to try and establish and understand what is driving this person.

The subconscious level is where the drivers and emotions come from. It is the emotional filter that the person is using to drive the importance of this story or project that you are talking about.

To have the person share more and for you to be able to see beyond the facts and data, you will need to turn off your inner voice and seek more to understand. As the person is talking, consider why they are telling you this, why is it important to them and where is this focus coming from.

If you are going to ask questions, Steven Covey (7 Habits of highly Effective People), suggests responding with a focus on how someone feels not on the facts. Replay them and wait for further information. "You feel that … can you tell me more?"

Strategic workshops

Clients don't seek solutions but are more often looking for partnerships that can guide them towards achieving their strategic goals. A recommendation is to instigate strategic workshops with your clients and or potential clients. Strategic workshops can serve as a powerful tool to foster collaboration, co-creation and deeper alignment with clients.

Strategic workshops are more than just meetings. They are structured sessions designed to bring together the expertise of the sales team and the insights of the client. The aim is to collaboratively explore challenges, brainstorm solutions, and chart out a roadmap for implementation and success.

Strategic Workshops raise your status in the customer's eyes, especially for those key accounts or strategic target accounts. It is your opportunity to separate yourself from other providers and demonstrate a distinctive dominance and competitive advantage. More about that in Force 4! Here are some other positive aspects of running strategic workshops:

Co-Creation: Unlike traditional sales pitches where solutions are presented, strategic workshops involve the client in the solution-creation process. This ensures that the solution is tailored to the client's unique needs and challenges, increasing the likelihood of adoption and success.

Building Stronger Relationships: Workshops provide an opportunity for face-to-face interaction, fostering a deeper understanding and building trust. Clients feel valued and involved, strengthening the bond between the sales team and the client.

Gaining a Competitive Edge: In a busy marketplace, offering strategic workshops can differentiate your offering from competitors. It positions your company as a thought leader and a trusted partner, not just a solution provider.

Uncovering Upsell and Cross-Sell Opportunities: As you delve deeper into the client's challenges and aspirations during the workshop, there's potential to identify additional areas where your product or service can add value, leading to upsell or cross-sell opportunities.

Reducing Implementation Barriers: By involving clients in the solution design process, you're also preparing them for implementation. They become familiar with the solution, its benefits, and how it fits into their ecosystem, reducing resistance and barriers when it's time to roll it out. Also, these workshops tend to involve a wider set of stakeholders and therefore reduce late-cycle concerns, objections and obstacles.

I have seen in the past that as part of product development, clients are asked for meetings to help develop the product further. This is not a bad idea, but it is often sold to the client in a way of helping the vendor, the Strategic Workshop is the opposite, it is a sold as a way to help the client.

Conducting Effective Strategic Workshops

Here are some things to ensure that your strategic workshops are impactful. Firstly it's essential to approach them with a clear structure and purpose. Start by defining the objectives of the workshop. Are you looking to address a specific challenge, explore new market opportunities, or design a tailored solution?

Next, ensure that the right stakeholders from both sides are present. This might include decision-makers, end-users, technical experts, and anyone else who can provide valuable input. Think about your usual buyer types: Technical Buyer, Economic Buyer, User Buyers as a starting point. For many organisations that sell software and technology solutions there are different decision makers that sit in the strategic buyer category, so make sure you include some of those.

Facilitation is key. Consider bringing in an experienced facilitator who can guide the discussion, ensure that all voices are heard, and keep the workshop on track. Use a mix of presentations, brainstorming sessions, breakout groups, and feedback rounds to keep the workshop engaging and productive. These sessions are sales pitches and therefore don't consider that it should be run and driven by sales alone. Consider it as part of a team approach, one where you are going to learn a lot from, so include both client and non-client facing people to be in the group as well.

Lastly, always conclude with clear next steps. Whether it's a follow-up meeting, a prototype design, or an implementation plan, ensure that both parties leave with a clear understanding of what comes next.

Value Visualisation

The true essence of the sale was not what a product can do but the transformative impact it promises. This is where the art of value visualisation comes into play. Having looked at deep dive engagement, where the focus was on laying the foundation of trust and understanding with your clients. Now, it's time in the words of Jerry McGuire to 'Show Me the Money". Okay maybe a little extreme, but whether you are working with existing clients aiming at retention and upsell, or selling to a new prospect, it's about painting a picture so compelling that clients can almost touch, feel, and experience the positive shifts your solution promises to bring into their business.

Value visualisation is not about presenting abstract concepts or hypothetical scenarios. It's about translating the intangible into tangible, the abstract into concrete, and the potential into actual positive business outcomes (PBOs). It's not about showcasing the journey but the destination – a brighter, more efficient, and prosperous future for your clients.

In this chapter, we'll explore the nuances of value visualisation, delving into strategies that can be utilised to deliver greater success. From the undeniable power of ROI revelations to the strategic alignment with PBOs and the persuasive use of success stories, we'll uncover the tools and techniques that make value visualisation an indispensable part of your sales arsenal.

ROI Revelations

For decades, value-based selling has been heralded as the cornerstone of solution selling. Rooted in the principle of demonstrating clear, quantifiable benefits to clients, it has long been the go-to strategy for sales professionals worldwide. But in today's rapidly evolving landscape, amidst economic downturns and shifting market dynamics, merely understanding value-based selling isn't enough. It's time to challenge our assumptions, refine our approach, and elevate our game.

A Narrative not a metric

ROI, or Return on Investment, is more than just a metric; it's a narrative. It's the story of how an investment in your solution translates into tangible business benefits. It's about showcasing the monetary gains, efficiency improvements, and competitive advantages that your product promises. But, more importantly, it's about aligning these benefits with the specific goals, challenges, and aspirations of your clients.

Let's be real, clients are inundated with competing options, each promising transformative results and ROI's. In such a saturated market, merely stating that your product offers value isn't enough. You need to quantify that value and make it palpable. This is where ROI Revelations come into play.

But here's the twist: while traditional value-based selling often focuses on presenting numbers and percentages, ROI Revelations delve deeper. It's about weaving those numbers into a compelling narrative, one that resonates with the client's unique context. It's about not just presenting data but telling a story – a story of success, growth, and transformation.

As we embark on this exploration of ROI Revelations, let's challenge the traditional paradigms of value-based selling moving beyond generic value propositions and diving into tailored, client-centric ROI narratives that not only demonstrate value but also captivate, convince, and convert.

Crafting Your ROI Narrative

We all know that numbers speak volumes. But numbers, devoid of context, can often fall on deaf ears. The true power of ROI lies in showcasing impressive figures, yes but, you need to weave those figures into a narrative that resonates with your client's unique challenges and aspirations.

When crafting a compelling ROI narrative, consider the following key points on the following page:

Understand Your Client's Landscape:
Before diving into numbers, take a step back. Understand the industry your client operates in, their market position, their competitors, and the challenges they face. This understanding will serve as the backdrop for your ROI story.

Align with Client Goals:
Every client has specific goals, whether it's expanding market share, improving operational efficiency or enhancing customer experience. Tailor your ROI narrative to show how your solution directly contributes to achieving these goals.

Quantify Tangible Benefits:
This is where you get into the nitty-gritty. Break down the tangible benefits your solution offers. Whether it's cost savings, increased revenue, or reduced operational downtime, ensure you have concrete figures to back up your claims.

Highlight Intangible Benefits:
While tangible benefits are crucial you shouldn't underestimate the power of intangible benefits like improved brand reputation, enhanced customer loyalty or better employee morale. These might be harder to quantify, but they can be equally compelling in your ROI narrative, especially to different departments and stakeholders in the clients business.

Use Real-world Examples:
Nothing reinforces an ROI narrative better than real-world success stories. Share case studies or testimonials of clients who've seen significant returns after implementing your solution. These stories serve as proof of your claims and add credibility to your narrative.

Address Potential Concerns:
Every ROI narrative will face scepticism. Anticipate potential concerns or objections your client might have and address them proactively in your narrative. Whether it's concerns about implementation time, integration challenges, or scalability, tackle them head-on.

Make It Personal:
Lastly, remember that every client is unique. Avoid generic ROI templates. Personalise your narrative to resonate with the specific individual or team you're addressing. This personal touch can make all the difference in making your ROI narrative stand out.

In the age of information overload, where clients are bombarded with sales pitches daily, a well-crafted ROI narrative can be your differentiator. It's about showcasing the value, whilst making that value felt, understood, and appreciated.

As you refine your approach to ROI Revelations, remember that at its core, it's a blend of art and science – the art of storytelling combined with the science of data-driven insights.

Positive Business Outcomes (PBOs)

Value Based selling has been an important aspect in selling to businesses and Gary Gaskill in his 2018 book discusses focusing on Business Outcomes and value drivers. Where this can mean ROI, it can be enhanced further and be more about demonstrating Positive Business Outcomes (PBOs).

PBOs provide a holistic view of the value derived from a solution, encompassing both tangible and intangible benefits. They go beyond the traditional ROI metrics, diving deeper into the broader business impact. For instance, while ROI might focus on immediate cost savings or efficiency gains, PBOs look at how a solution can transform business operations, open new market opportunities, or enhance customer relationships.

Remember our discussion on ROI Revelations? Think of ROI as a subset of the broader PBO framework. While ROI gives you the numbers, PBOs provide the narrative – the story of transformation and growth.

In the context of SaaS and tech based sales, PBOs become even more critical. As the tech landscape is dynamic, with rapid technological advancements and evolving customer needs we have already summised that the clients are looking for a strategic partner who understands their long-term vision and can guide them towards achieving it. By aligning your solution with their PBOs, you position yourself as that trusted partner.

Uncovering Value

Ok, this book isn't about teaching questioning techniques, but there are 4 question types that are important to bring into the fold to ensure the team can uncover build out the value.

4Q Questioning

Understanding that we need to engage the customer's heart and mind, and get past the fast logic brain stage, we need our questioning techniques to get through the barriers and have the customer open-up and share both business needs and personal needs as well. This is especially essential when making larger sales.

The 4Q's are an awesome tool to help you do this. The 4Q's are:

- Background Questions
- Problem Questions
- Value Questions
- Impact Questions

These are named to provide instant clarity of what they are about, no need for fancy jargon here.

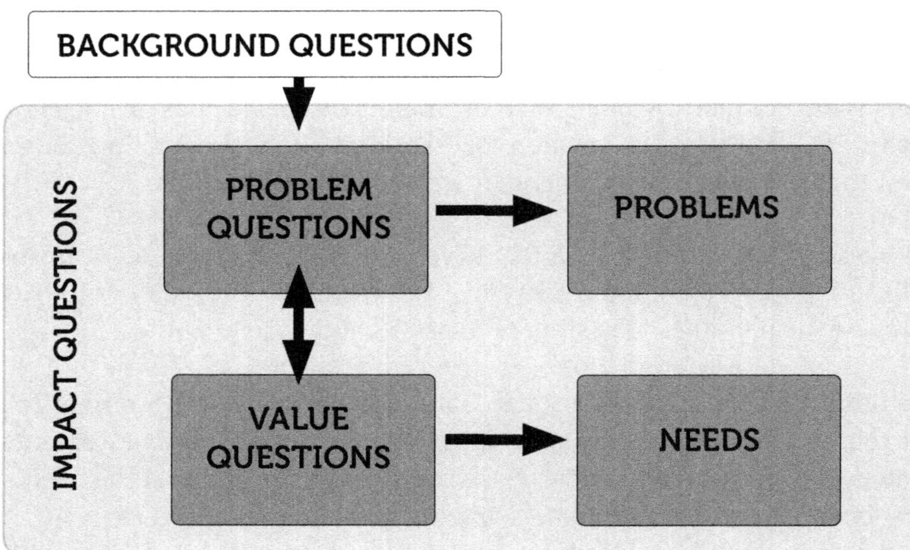

The 4Q's are 4 very powerful and useful question types that help lead the customer to share with their problems and needs that your product and services can solve.

It is not a flow diagram and it is not a process. You can ask any of the questions in any order. Don't feel that you need to get all the Background questions out, then all the problems and then move onto Value. Conversations are not like that and therefore your questions shouldn't work like that either.

Yes, it makes sense to roll onto some as part of the conversation, but do not limit yourself, go with the flow of the conversation but make sure you are influencing the clients mind throughout.

Background Questions

Background questions provide just that. They focus on establishing the facts about the company, situation, or topic or to confirm some data that may be of interest. In today's world the customer expects you to have completed some research and not be asking time-wasting questions. Top sellers may still ask background questions, but usually utilise them to clarify some information or to move the customer into a topic they want to explore. Background questions have little to no influence over the customer's thinking.

Some examples:

> *"how many employees do you have"*
> *"What's your current labour turnover rate"*
> *"What are your strategic priorities at the moment"*

The most important part of Background questions is that they need to get to Level 2 – a much more well-reasoned response.

Problem Questions (building the case for change)

In "Insight Selling" by Mike Schultz and John Doerr, it's highlighted that top salespeople today shift away from the traditional deep needs analysis you find in consultative or solution selling. Instead, they offer insights and guide the customer to the solution, as referenced in Force 1: Disruptive Mindset.

Enter the concept of problem questions, a subset of the 4Q's. These aren't about gathering mere facts like background questions. They aim to engage the customer mentally, drawing out their opinions or feelings about challenges they're grappling with. This method starts to connect with the customer on an emotional level, immediately elevating their response to Level 2 brain activity, reminiscent of what we discussed under Active Listening.

Crafting effective problem questions involves leaning on emotion-evoking words and framing them in a 'Leading' question style. Consider using words like...

worried	*nervous*
afraid	*alarmed*
difficult	*Awkward*
frustrated	*apprehensive*
Confident	*disappointed*
dissatisfied	*doubt*
bothered	*annoyed*

Again as described in Force 1, we need to lead the customer to your solution so focus on asking questions that your products and services can fix.

Some example questions are:

> "how worried are you that your team are wasting too much time on paperwork?'
> "do you find it difficult finding the information you need?"
> "How frustrating is it that your sales team struggle to build close relationships with you customers?"

Value Based Questions (moving to a solution mindset)
After hearing the customer's challenges, you might be tempted to dive in, explaining how your products and services can address them. Don't! It's premature!

Diving into solutions before the customer expresses their desired outcome places them in a critical mode towards your pitch. Essentially, you'd be leading with a solution not to the solution. The likelihood of your pitch aligning perfectly with their mental image of the ideal solution is slim. This misalignment can generate reservations, such as, *"I can see why some people want that, but..."* or *"That seems more elaborate than what I had in mind".*

Value questions play a crucial role here. They help sustain the customer's engagement, transitioning them from discussing the present challenges to envisioning a brighter, solution-filled future. At this juncture, it's vital to keep the dialogue inquisitive rather than dictating how you can assist.

However, this doesn't imply you become a passive participant. The key is to pose thought-provoking questions that subtly hint at potential solutions. By doing so, you allow them to vocalize the benefits they seek. In neuroscience, this strategy is termed "Priming". Through cooperative suggestions, you can guide customers into a forward-thinking frame of mind, where they visualize various facets of the potential solution.

Use phrases such as *"if you could...."* Or *"if you had a way ..."*

Again this is a subtle art form. It is not "If you had our Widget 2000 how would that help" or "if you could use our Widget what difference would that make?" The answer lies in what the feature does, more it's functionality, not what it is.

Consider a client of ours who offers an HR information system with an array of impressive features. One notable feature focuses on streamlining the onboarding process for new hires. This is traditionally a tedious aspect of HR, involving sending numerous forms to incoming employees, gathering details ranging from personal information, right to work and references. Moreover, coordinating with internal departments like IT and facilities is essential to set up emails, ensure building access, provide laptops, and more. Customers commonly encounter challenges such as incomplete or incorrectly filled forms, expired passports, or paperwork getting misplaced between departments.

Here is an extract of part of the conversation as an example:

> Background Q: *"can you describe to me your current onboarding process of new hires?"*
> Problem Q: *"are you concerned that your team are wasting too much time chasing up paperwork"*
> Customer: *"yes, they can spend ages typing up the letters and following up to get all the information together"*
> Value Q: *"I see, so if you could automate that process, what difference would that make?"*

Value Questions emphasize the prospective solution's advantages, nudging the customer to ponder the merits of automated documentation. This shifts the customer's perspective to envisioning a future benefit. While the customer recognizes the salesperson's intent (given their product offers such a solution), the dialogue feels more cooperative rather than overtly sales-driven.

Crafting a Compelling Argument for Change

The fourth Q is Impact Questions. Impact questions amplify the severity of the existing problem or the potential benefits of a solution. These questions furnish concrete metrics to underscore the three pivotal questions: Why Change? Why Now? Why Us? When engaging with businesses, especially cost-sensitive ones, exposing the tangible repercussions of the status quo and the tangible advantages of the proposed system can make it easier for your point of contact to advocate for the solution among other stakeholders.

There are five different areas you could consider drawing impact questions from:

1. Time
2. Money
3. People
4. Workflow / Processes
5. Strategy / Plans

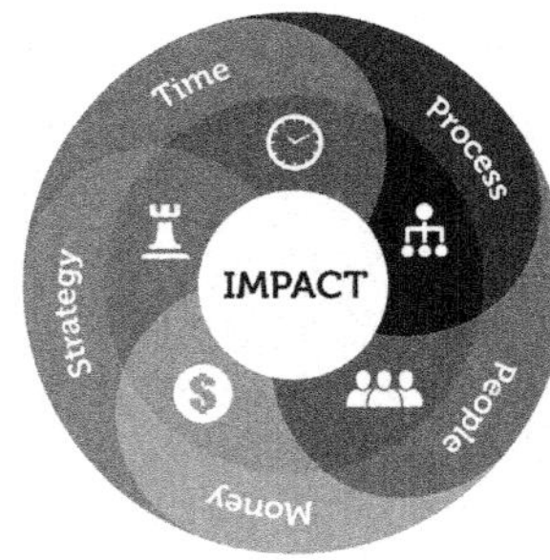

Time & Money
While time and Money are usually the most evident aspects, they're often the primary focus during the initial stages of the sales conversation. Most business stakeholders, especially those at executive levels like CFOs, prioritize saving time and optimizing budgets. You might delve into questions such as, "How much time is currently spent on this?" or "What financial impact is this issue causing?" These types of queries might be anticipated by the client, especially if they've pre-calculated these losses, making these aspects crucial to your discussion. On the flip side, exploring the potential benefits like, "How much time will this solution recover?" or "What financial advantages will this offer?" can provide a balanced perspective.

However, it's essential to remember that your competitors are likely highlighting these same two benefits. While time and finances are invaluable, they're not the sole aspects that matter. To truly set yourself apart, delve into the realms of the other three areas: strategy, people, and processes.

People
When considering **people** as an impact question, you can ask your customer things like: "Who else is affected by this?" and "Will that also impact you customers?". Very rarely is a problem or benefit limited to just one part of

your company. The more people that are impacted, the bigger the problem and the higher priority it will become to get it solved as soon as possible. A cut on the finger can be covered up with a bandage; a wound that is bleeding from five different spots needs immediate attention.

In addition, impact on other people, especially customers, gets the ear of different people in an organisation. If you contact is going to need additional sign off, other members of the leadership team will be more prone to listen and act if it affects customers.

Strategy

Strategy questions could involve asking what other projects are being delayed, shelved, or cancelled because of the problem at hand, or what are the future goals and objectives and how will this impact those going forward. This is a far-reaching question that might not immediately be apparent depending on the level of responsibility of the person you are engaging with. You could ask "What is this stopping you from doing?"

Process

Consider the impact in terms of Processes or Workflow. Does the problem or need have additional impacts on these elements of the business. Depending on your products and services this might have a larger or lesser of an impact, but when you start looking at what is affected you will be surprised at how you can extend the size of the pain and gain into these areas. Consider 'What areas are being held up, what blockages occur, will this help streamline certain aspects of the workflow?' Below is an example of workflow and processes issues from the previous example for the HR system provider but this time with the impact questions added:

> *Background Q: "can you describe to me your current onboarding process of new hires?"*
> *Problem Q: "are you concerned that your team are wasting too much time chasing up paperwork"*
> *Customer: "yes, they can spend ages typing up the letters and follow up to get all the information together"*
> *Impact Q: "what negative impact does that have on the new hires?"*
> *Impact Q: "If the paperwork is late coming back –does that affect any other departments?"*
> *Impact Q: "because they are sales hires, does that have a knock-on effect in terms of sales targets and revenue?"*

Value Q: "I see, so if you could automate that process, what difference would that make?"
Impact Q: "how much time do you think that would save?"
Impact Q: "would that also help with your future recruitment drive"
Impact Q: "and what about employee engagement – would you see that go up for your own team and that of new recruits?"

Asking impact questions helps the customer realise that the problem is bigger than it appears on the surface and can move it to a more strategic conversation rather than tactical. This is the platform on which you will build the case for change, which is the linchpin in getting a customer to pull the trigger and make the decision to buy.

On the face of it, questions are simple, ask the customer what they want and give it to them. Yes, if you want to be an average salesperson! Top salespeople know that you can use questions to lead the customer to believe they are engineering a solution which just so happens to be exactly what they are selling!

True value-based selling will require you to link your solution at multiple levels of the organisation, such as; Business Objectives , how does this attribute to the organisations strategic objectives, departmental objectives, how does it actually help, and KPI's, how does it help achieve and deliver real performance metrics.

Metrics are more than ROI

Building metrics is more than providing a return on Investment. When you become more engaged in the conversation with the customer and the conversations turn to be more about the impact of the solution, you change the dynamic of the sale and your relationship.

Building Champions

One of the aspects in business to business (b2b) sales is that the person you are dealing with, more often will need to sell the solution internally to the other stakeholders. Working through the impact, and building out the metrics, provides them with the tools they need to gain buy-in to the solution, but also moves you into more of a coaching relationship. You are helping build out their personal wins and therefore reinforcing your relationships.

Move from Tactical to Strategic

Focusing on the impacts of the solution, rather than the features and operation of the product, migrates the sale from being a tactical purchase, or a product acquisition, to a strategic project that impacts not only the department by far wider across the business. It changes the conversation from being about what to do to fix things today, to a longer, future focused perspective.

Shift from Price to Value

The focus also moves away from price and how much it costs, to the value the business will gain from the having the solution, both in terms of the removal of the pain and benefits they will gain. Value will be measured differently by different departments, and therefore remember to utilise the variety of impact questions.

Opens doors

Having metrics will raise interest in a lot more people than the person you are dealing with. Yes, the Economic Buyer will be interested, but also so will a wider audience, both within the existing customers' business and for you other prospects. When you want to get higher and wider across the existing organisation, these metrics will be important to demonstrate the impact you have had already, and doors will suddenly be open to you, as people will want to learn more.

Leverage PBOs into Conversations

So, how can a sales professional leverage PBOs into their client conversations?

Understand the Client's Big Picture: Before diving into the features of your solution, take a step back and understand the client's overarching business goals. This will come from your Insight gathering and research. What are they trying to achieve in the next 5 years? What challenges are they anticipating?

Align with Strategic Objectives: Once you have a clear understanding of their goals, align your solution with these objectives. Show them how your product or service can be a catalyst in achieving their PBOs.

Narrate Success Stories: Share case studies or testimonials that highlight the PBOs achieved by similar businesses using your solution. These real-world examples provide concrete evidence of the transformative impact your product can have.

Collaborate and Co-create: Engage clients in collaborative sessions, much like the strategic workshops we discussed earlier. These sessions can be instrumental in co-creating a roadmap to achieve the desired PBOs.

Incorporating PBOs into your sales approach not only strengthens your value proposition but also fosters deeper, more meaningful client relationships. It shifts the conversation from a transactional sale to a strategic partnership, ensuring long-term success for both parties.

Real Word Evidence

While data-driven insights and ROI revelations are crucial, they often lack the emotional resonance that drives decision-making. A well-crafted success story is more than just a testimonial, it's a narrative that showcases the transformative impact of your product on similar businesses. It provides concrete evidence of value delivery, bridging the gap between abstract benefits and tangible results. But more than that, it humanises the sales process. It allows potential clients to envision themselves in the narrative, to see their challenges mirrored and to imagine the triumph of finding a solution.

Think about the times you've made purchases based on recommendations or reviews. There's comfort in knowing someone else has walked the path before you and found value in their journey. Success stories serve a similar purpose for your solution. They offer a window into the experiences of peers, acting as a beacon for prospective clients navigating the decision-making maze.

To effectively leverage success stories in your sales approach, it's crucial to tailor them to your audience. A generic success story might pique interest, but a story that resonates with the specific challenges, industry, and objectives of the client you're engaging with will strike a chord. It's about finding that common thread that binds the client's current situation with the success narrative you're presenting.

Moreover, the emphasis on Positive Business Outcomes (PBOs) cannot be understated. These outcomes, as we've discussed earlier, are the ultimate indicators of value realisation. A compelling success story will seamlessly weave these PBOs into the narrative, highlighting the journey from challenge to solution to tangible business benefits.

3-Step Story Telling

Storytelling is often considered an ancient art form, used for millennia to convey ideas, share knowledge, and inspire action. In the realm of sales, storytelling becomes a powerful tool to connect with clients on an emotional level, making the abstract tangible and the complex comprehensible. But your clients don't want a long drawn out story, they need to relate, connect and see themselves successful in it. To keep it on point below is a 3-point plan for you storytelling:

1. **Every story has a Protagonist:** Every story needs a central character, and in our context this character is often a business or an individual facing challenges similar to those of your potential client. By crafting a protagonist that mirrors the client's situation, you create an immediate connection, allowing them to see themselves in the narrative.

2. **Building a Narrative Arc**: Like any good story, there should be a beginning, middle, and end. Start with the challenges faced by the protagonist (the client's challenges), delve into the journey of discovering and implementing your solution, and conclude with the transformative results achieved. If you prefer a structure for this check out the Hypnotic Heartbeat in Force 1.

3. **Emphasising Emotional Touchpoints**: While data and facts are crucial, it's the emotional resonance that often drives decision-making. Highlight moments of frustration, the relief of finding a solution, and the joy of achieving desired outcomes. These emotional touchpoints make your story memorable and relatable.

Bring the Story to Life in Visuals

Visual elements, such as graphs and charts, can further enhance the impact of your success story. They offer a visual representation of the journey, adding credibility and making the information more digestible.

But remember, it's not just about presenting data; it's about telling a story. Craft your success stories in a narrative format that takes the reader on a journey, making the content engaging and memorable.

Infographics: These are a great way to represent complex data in an easily understandable format. For instance, showing the growth trajectory of a client before and after implementing your solution can be powerfully conveyed through a well-designed infographic.

Charts and Graphs: While numbers and percentages are informative, visualising this data through charts and graphs makes it more accessible. It allows potential clients to quickly grasp the magnitude of change and the benefits achieved.

Videos and Animations: A short video testimonial from satisfied clients or an animation explaining how your solution works can be more engaging than written content. It offers a dynamic way to convey information and can be especially effective in demonstrating product features or showcasing client success stories.

Interactive Demos: For software solutions, an interactive demo can be invaluable. It allows potential clients to experience the product first hand, understand its features, and envision how it might fit into their operations.

Incorporating storytelling and visual elements into your sales approach is not just about making your pitch more engaging; it's about making it more effective. It's about moving beyond mere facts and figures to create a compelling narrative that resonates with clients, allowing them to see the value of your solution not just in terms of ROI but in terms of real-world impact.

By weaving together data, narrative, and visuals, you create a holistic sales approach that speaks to both the head and the heart, ensuring that your message is not only heard but also felt.

Direct from the horse's mouth

Lastly, consider the power of peer-to-peer conversations. If circumstances allow, connecting potential clients with those who've provided testimonials can be invaluable. These conversations offer insights that go beyond the written word, further reinforcing the value of your solution. Failing that, recorded video testimonials are also extremely powerful.

In essence, success stories are more than just endorsements; they are narratives of transformation. By effectively integrating them into your sales approach, you not only showcase the value of your solution but also build trust and credibility with your clients.

Incorporating success stories into your sales approach adds depth to your value proposition. It provides clients with real-world evidence of what your solution can achieve, making the decision-making process more straightforward and more compelling.

Flexible & Tailored Solutions

Selling software and technology is not about selling a product, it's about selling a solution that fits seamlessly into the client's unique ecosystem. This approach is the very essence of client-centricity.

For new prospects, the allure of a solution that feels customised to them can be the deciding factor in choosing your product over a competitor's. It signals a deep understanding of their specific challenges and a willingness to adapt to their needs. For existing customers, tailored solutions and flexibility in terms and offerings can be the difference between a routine renewal and an upsell or expansion opportunity. It reinforces the message that as their business evolves, so does your commitment to serving them optimally.

But what does it truly mean to offer flexible and tailored solutions in a SaaS context, after all the platform is the platform right? Well yes and no. It's a blend of adaptive product offerings that can be moulded to fit unique client requirements and flexible terms that accommodate varying business constraints and growth stages. It's about striking the right balance between standardisation for scalability and customisation for individual client satisfaction.

As we delve deeper into this topic, we'll explore the nuances of adaptive offerings, the importance of flexible terms, and how these strategies not only drive sales but also foster long-term client relationships in both acquisition and retention phases.

Adaptive Offerings

While certain challenges may be industry-wide, the nuances of how they manifest in each business can vary widely. This is where the power of adaptive offerings comes into play.

Imagine walking into a boutique where every outfit is custom-made to fit you perfectly, as opposed to a one-size-fits-all approach. The former not only ensures a better fit but also makes you feel valued and understood. This is the essence of adaptive offerings in the tech world.

By providing modular or customizable solutions, you're sending a clear message to potential clients: "We understand that your business is unique, and we're here to offer a solution tailored to your specific needs." This approach not only enhances the perceived value of your product but also establishes a deeper connection with the client.

Imagine a prospect in the healthcare sector looking for a CRM solution. While the core functionalities of CRM remain consistent across industries, the healthcare sector might have specific needs related to patient data privacy, appointment scheduling, or integration with medical record systems. An adaptive offering in this context would mean tailoring your CRM to address these unique requirements, making it not just a CRM, but a healthcare-specific CRM solution.

For existing customers, adaptability can manifest in the form of modular add-ons or features that they can opt into as their business grows or changes. For instance, a retail client using your e-commerce platform might initially only need basic online storefront capabilities. But as they expand, they might require advanced inventory management or integration with a new payment gateway. Being able to offer these features as adaptive modules ensures that your solution grows with your client, cementing the relationship further.

But how do you ensure that your adaptive offerings are hitting the mark? It goes back to the principles of deep dive engagement and value visualization. By actively listening to clients, understanding their pain points, and visualizing the value your solution brings, you can craft offerings that resonate deeply.

Incorporating adaptive offerings into your sales strategy is more than just a selling point; it's a commitment. A commitment to understanding, to flexibility, and to delivering value in its truest sense. And in a highly competitive world, such a commitment can be the difference between a missed opportunity and a long-term partnership. Adaptability isn't just about the product; it's also about the mindset. Cultivating a culture within your sales team that values deep client understanding, continuous feedback loops, and a willingness to go the extra mile can be the differentiator. It's about listening more than speaking, understanding more than assuming, and crafting more than selling. Things we have spoken about already in all 3 forces so far.

Flexible Terms

In an ideal world, every prospect would have the budget, readiness, and eagerness to invest in your solution without hesitation. But the reality of sales, especially in a challenging economic climate, is far from this utopia. Economic downturns, budget constraints, and shifting priorities can often make clients hesitant to commit, especially to long-term contracts or significant upfront costs. This is where the power of flexible terms comes into play.

Flexible terms are not just about pricing adjustments; they're a strategic tool that demonstrates your genuine commitment to the client's success. By offering varied pricing models, payment terms, or contract durations, you're essentially telling your client, "We understand your challenges, and we're here to work with you."

For new prospects, flexibility can be the bridge that turns a 'maybe later' into a 'let's start now.' For instance, a start-up might see the immense value in your solution but is wary of the financial commitment. By offering them a tiered pricing model that scales with their growth or a trial period to test the waters, you're reducing their perceived risk and making the decision easier.

For existing customers, flexible terms can be a lifeline in turbulent times. Consider a long-standing client hit hard by an economic downturn. They value your solution but are struggling with cash flow. By renegotiating contract terms, offering temporary discounts, or even transitioning them to a 'lite' version of your product, you're not just retaining a client; you're building loyalty that will pay dividends when the tide turns.

However, it's essential to strike a balance. While flexibility is a strength, it shouldn't come at the cost of undermining the value of your solution. It's about finding that sweet spot where you're accommodating the client's needs without devaluing your offering.

Crafting Flexible Terms

The terms of engagement can often be as crucial as the product itself. While the features and functionalities of a software solution are undoubtedly vital, the terms under which a client engages with a provider can make or break a deal. This is where the art of crafting flexible terms comes into play. Crafting flexible terms is a strategic approach that demonstrates your commitment to client-centricity, showing that you are willing to adapt to meet their unique needs and circumstances.

Understanding Client Constraints

Before diving into the specifics, it's essential to understand why flexibility matters so much to clients. In a rapidly evolving business landscape, companies face uncertainties ranging from market dynamics to regulatory changes. Long-term commitments can feel daunting, especially if they come with rigid terms that don't account for potential shifts in the client's circumstances.

Before you can offer flexible terms, you need to have a deep understanding of your client's constraints and requirements. This involves active listening and deep dive engagement, which we discussed in the previous chapter. By understanding their budget constraints, contract preferences, and any other specific requirements, you can tailor your terms to better align with their needs.

Varied Pricing Models:

Another critical area is pricing. Traditional fixed-price models might not always resonate with every client. Consider introducing tiered pricing, usage-based pricing, or even performance-based models. For instance, a client who's unsure about the potential ROI from your solution might be more inclined to engage if there's a performance-based pricing model in place, where they pay more only when they derive more value. The key is to provide options that allow clients to choose the model that best fits their budget and usage needs.

Flexible Payment Terms:

Another aspect of flexibility is in the payment terms. This could mean offering different payment schedules, such as monthly, quarterly, or annual payments. For clients who may be facing budget constraints, especially in a slow economy, this flexibility can be the difference between a closed deal and a lost opportunity.

Adaptable Contract Durations:

One of the primary areas where flexibility is sought is in contract duration. While long-term contracts can offer stability for both the provider and the client, they can also feel restrictive. Offering a range of contract durations, from monthly to multi-year, allows clients to choose a term that aligns with their comfort level and business projections. For instance, start-ups might prefer shorter durations due to the volatile nature of their business, while established enterprises might opt for longer terms in exchange for better pricing.

Exit Clauses and Renewals

The terms under which a client can exit a contract or renew it are equally crucial. While it's standard to have penalties for early termination, consider offering a more lenient exit clause for specific circumstances, such as significant business downturns. On the renewal front, automatic renewals can be convenient, but it's essential to ensure clients are given ample notice and the option to opt-out.

Customisation and Integration Terms

For many clients, the real value of a solution lies in its ability to integrate seamlessly with their existing systems. Ensure that your terms accommodate custom integrations, API access, and other technical requirements that clients might have. This not only adds value but also positions your solution as an integral part of the client's tech ecosystem.

Building Trust and Long-Term Relationships:

By offering flexible terms, you are sending a message to your clients that you are willing to work with them and adapt to their needs. This builds trust and lays the foundation for a long-term relationship. It shows that you are not just interested in making a sale, but in ensuring that your solution truly meets their needs and adds value to their business.

Crafting flexible terms is a strategic approach that demonstrates client-centricity and adaptability. It involves understanding client constraints, offering varied pricing models, flexible payment terms, and adaptable contract durations. By doing so, you build trust, foster long-term relationships, and position yourself as a client-centric organization that is ready to meet the unique needs of each client. In my mind, flexibility and adaptive offerings should reduce the need for discount and provides the sales team / customer success team better options to discuss with clients the options rather than negotiate terms.

Driving Lifetime Client Value

The true measure of success isn't just about acquiring new customers, it's about nurturing and growing them over time. It's about transcending transactional relationships and forging genuine partnerships that stand the test of time. This is where the concept of driving lifetime customer value takes centre stage.

As you've journeyed through the disruptive mindset and harnessed the power of insight agility, you've laid the groundwork for a client-centric approach. But what does it truly mean to be client-centric in the long run? It means understanding that the sale is just the beginning of a potentially lifelong relationship. It means continuously striving to deliver on the promises made during the sales process and ensuring that customers derive real, tangible value from your solution at every stage of their journey.

This chapter delves into the essence of driving lifetime customer value, a philosophy that goes beyond customer retention. It's about proactive engagement, understanding evolving needs, and being a steadfast partner in your customer's growth story. From the initial onboarding to ensuring they see the promised value, and then identifying opportunities for growth, every step is crucial. It's a holistic approach, one that requires a blend of strategy, empathy, and foresight.

So, as we continue to navigate through this pivotal aspect of the Five Force Model, remember: in the world of recurring revenue sales, your customers' success is your success. Driving lifetime value is the key to unlocking sustainable growth and unparalleled competitive advantage.

Understanding Lifetime Value

Lifetime Value, often abbreviated as LTV, is a metric that represents the total net profit a company expects to earn from a single customer throughout their relationship. It's a projection of all the value a business would derive from the entire future relationship with a customer. Rather than looking at a single transaction or a brief period of engagement, LTV takes a long-term view, encompassing the entire customer journey from acquisition to eventual churn.

The concept of LTV is not new, but its importance has been magnified in the digital age, especially in subscription-based models and, according to Bain & Company, increasing customer retention by 5% can lead to profits increasing by 25%-95%, especially when reviewing the cost of client acquisition. It provides businesses with a lens to view customer relationships not just as a series of transactions, but as ongoing partnerships that deliver value over time. By understanding and optimizing LTV, companies can make informed decisions about customer acquisition, retention, and growth strategies.

Several thought leaders have delved deep into the intricacies of LTV. For instance, in his book "Contagious: How to Build Word of Mouth in the Digital Age," Jonah Berger discusses the ripple effect of positive customer experiences and how they can amplify LTV. Similarly, in "Hacking Growth," authors Sean Ellis and Morgan Brown explore how companies such as Airbnb, LinkedIn, and Dropbox use data-driven marketing techniques to maximize LTV and drive sustainable growth.

In essence, Lifetime Value is a reflection of the sustained value a customer brings to a business. It underscores the importance of not just winning customers but nurturing and growing them, ensuring that they remain valuable partners in the long run.

The concept of Lifetime Value underscores a fundamental shift in the way businesses approach customer relationships. It's no longer about a single transaction or even a series of transactions. Instead, it's about the entire journey, the holistic experience, and the sustained value derived over time. This perspective necessitates a move beyond the initial sale. But what does it truly mean to go "Beyond the Sale"?

While the sale might be the starting point of a customer's journey with your product or service, it's merely the tip of the iceberg. The real value, both for your business and for the customer, lies in what happens next. It's about nurturing that relationship, understanding evolving needs, and ensuring that your product continues to deliver value as those needs change. Let's delve deeper into this concept and explore how you can effectively transition from a sale to a lasting partnership.

Beyond the Sale

The journey with your client doesn't end once the sale is closed; in fact, it's just the beginning. This new chapter in the customer relationship is where the true essence of your company's commitment shines through. While it's one thing to make grand promises during the sales process, it's the delivery of those promises post-sale that sets exceptional companies apart.

Before we get into the core elements of driving greater customer success, here are some key core elements:

Consistent Communication	It's essential to maintain regular touchpoints with your clients. These aren't just routine check-ins but genuine opportunities to understand their experience with your product. Are they facing any challenges? Is there something they wish the product could do? By proactively reaching out, you can pre-empt potential issues, ensuring that your clients always feel valued and heard.
Be More Than Just a Vendor	Providing top-notch customer support is a given in today's competitive landscape, but what if you could offer more? Think of yourself as a consultant and partner. Offer strategic guidance, share best practices, and provide insights that can help them maximise the value they get from your product.
Product Evolution	To stay relevant, it's crucial that your product adapts to industry trends and, more importantly, to specific feedback from your clients. This commitment to evolution not only enhances your product's value but also showcases your dedication to your clients' success.
Empower with Education	Consider offering webinars, workshops, and training sessions. These resources can help your clients unlock the full potential of your product, and it's a testament to your expertise in the domain.
Celebrate Every Milestone	Every time your client achieves a significant milestone with your product, take a moment to celebrate it. It could be a feature in a case study, a shoutout on your company's social media, or even a simple congratulatory email. These gestures go a long way in fostering goodwill and reinforcing the partnership ethos.

In essence, going beyond the sale means transitioning from transactional interactions to building transformative relationships. These deep-rooted relationships not only ensure customer retention but also open doors for upselling, cross-selling, and garnering referrals. It's a symbiotic relationship where both parties thrive, truly embodying the spirit of driving lifetime customer value.

Optimisation and Engagement

A pivotal aspect to enhance within the Customer Success phase of the sales journey is establishing a framework around the contract lifecycle, emphasizing long-term value. This encompasses onboarding, promoting user engagement, cultivating value, and facilitating contract renewals.

Around that lifecycle, there will be 4 core elements:

Time to Live – onboarding the customer and getting them set up successfully on the system.

Time to Value – uncovering metrics and proving value.

Time to Show - engaging the customer to discuss new features and what's possible.

Time to Grow – a strategic plan to expand the account whilst protecting existing revenue.

Quarterly Business Reviews

Quarterly Business Reviews (QBRs) are strategic touchpoints held typically held every three months between SaaS vendors and their clients. Of course, the primary purpose is to analyse product performance, align goals, and strategize on maximizing value from the software or service. In the domain of customer success, QBRs act as a platform to ensure that both the service provider and the client are on the same page, fostering mutual growth and understanding.

QBRs become essential to continually nurture the client relationship, ensuring the service provided meets evolving business needs, and proactively address any challenges that might arise. Effective QBRs not only strengthen customer loyalty but also increase the potential for contract renewals and upsells. They can spotlight opportunities for product improvements or highlight areas where clients may need additional training or support.

One of the challenges I have often experienced in QBRs is the lack of structure or focus. The call is often booked and acts more of a customer service, happiness call. It becomes even more difficult with longer-term clients, as everything is running smoothly and the CSM (customer success manager) doesn't have much to say or know where to take the call.

To provide some structure to the QBRs the diagram gives some consideration to the process.

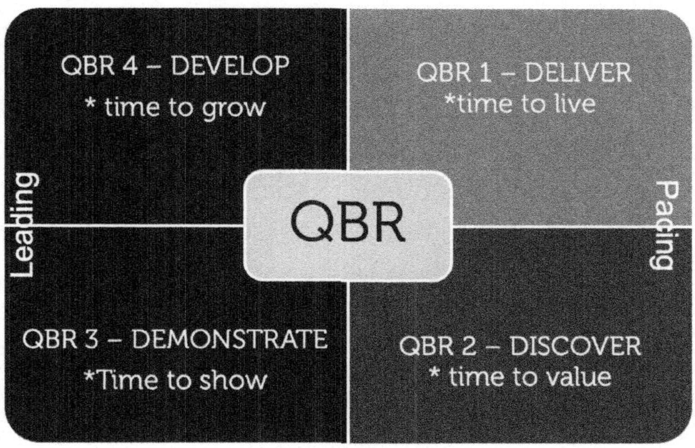

Having a clear roadmap of the four QBRs that are going to take place this year makes it easy for the management of the account. As you can see from the digram you could consider:

QBR 1:	Deliver - focused on delivering on the promises made and getting the client launched on the platform or live on the new services.
QBR 2:	Discover - focused on uncovering metrics, alignment of PBOs, and discovery conversations.
QBR 3:	Demonstrate - leveraged off the discovery in QBR 2, demonstrate new opportunities and capabilities from the platform.
QBR 4:	Develop - following the discussions from QBR 3, it's time for renewal, upsell and cross-sell.

Let's caveat that the above is only feasible if the client is seeing progress and is happy with the service and solution provided. If there's low user adoption or issues with the service, some of these QBR stages might be delayed.

Pacing and Leading

In the model you will see that QBR 1 and 2 are listed as 'Pacing', whilst 3 and 4 are 'Leading'. "Pacing" and "leading" are terms commonly associated with neuro-linguistic programming (NLP) and communication techniques, especially in the context of rapport-building and influencing. Here's what each term means:

Pacing:

In the context of NLP and communication, founded on the work by John Grinder and Richard Bandler, pacing refers to the act of matching and mirroring another person's behaviour, language, or emotional state. This can include mimicking body language, using similar vocabulary, and matching their pace, pitch and tone. The idea behind pacing is to create a sense of familiarity and rapport with the other person. When someone feels that you are "in sync" with them, it can foster trust and open lines of communication.

Leading:

Once rapport has been established through pacing, leading is the act of gradually introducing new behaviours, language, or emotional states with the expectation that the other person will follow or match you. The goal of leading is to guide the interaction or influence the other person in a desired direction. For example, if you've paced someone by matching their anxious behaviour and then gradually introduce calm behaviours, the idea is that they'll start to feel and act calmer in response to your leading. The idea therefore is that in QBR 1 and 2, the CSM is focusing their effort and energy to build rapport with the customer, following their lead and fostering trust. As they progress into QBR 3 and 4, they start to take the lead and influence their thoughts and actions.

As we dive into each of the 4 QBR's you will see how pacing and leading come into play. We will also look into this a little more in Force 5: Emotional Intelligence.

Time to Live

The initial phase after a sale is crucial. It's the period where your client transitions from the promises made during the sales process to the implementation of your product. This phase we refer to as the 'Time to Live (TtL)', is about onboarding, and implementing the solution to deliver on the promised functionality and to meet the client expectations.

The Onboarding Experience

Onboarding isn't just about technical integrations or setting up accounts. It's the first real taste your client gets of how it feels to work with your product and, by extension, your company. A smooth, efficient, and supportive onboarding process can set the tone for the entire relationship.

From the outset, it's essential to set clear expectations. What can the client expect in the coming days? What are the milestones? Who are their points of contact? By providing a roadmap, you alleviate any potential anxieties and set the stage for a structured onboarding process. What is important is to ensure that role and responsibilities are also established on both sides, your organisation and theirs.

While your product might be intuitive to you, remember that new clients might need guidance. Offering comprehensive training sessions ensures that they can harness the full power of your solution from day one. This not only speeds up their 'Time to Live' but also enhances their overall satisfaction.

During onboarding, clients might have numerous questions or face challenges. Ensure that they have direct channels to reach out for support. Whether it's a dedicated account manager, a helpline, or a chatbot, being accessible can make all the difference.

Use the onboarding phase as an opportunity to gather feedback. Are there areas where clients consistently face challenges? Is there a feature they wish they had? This feedback is invaluable. It not only helps improve the onboarding experience for future clients but can also provide insights into potential product enhancements.

Time to Value

As your clients settle into using your product, the journey from 'Time to Live' to 'Time to Value' becomes the focal point of their experience. This transition is critical, it's where the promises made during the sales process and the expectations set during onboarding start to materialize into tangible benefits.

'Time to Value' (TtV) is all about realisation and recognition. It's the period where clients start to see the impact of your solution on their operations, efficiency, and bottom line. They begin to understand not just the functionalities of your product, but its role in driving their business forward.

Get in Early

Uncovering Value as part of the QBR process it easier if you schedule the evaluation process during the setup phase. I often find that if you book the date for an evaluation meeting at the initial kick-off session, the customer is primed and prepped for it. Not only that, but it also sets expectations for the client that they will see benefits and returns by a certain date, for example week 12.

Let's examine this from a psychological perspective. How does it differ when you ask a customer about the product's benefits or value 9 months after implementation compared to just 3 months in? It boils down to the customer's perception of your intent. At the 3-month mark, the customer is likely to feel that you're genuinely curious and aiming to provide value. However, by the 9-month point, they might suspect you're inquiring due to an upcoming renewal. The answers that you receive will therefore be linked to what they believe is your intention.

Therefore, three months in, the customer feels you are inquiring on their behalf. If they were part of the initial purchasing decision, they'd likely offer positive feedback, wanting to demonstrate the product's beneficial impact on the company. They'll be more proactive in presenting results and determining the ROI. However, by the ninth month, they might understate the product's value, but will be concerned that sharing them with you could influence your stance on the renewal negotiations.

Revealing the Perceived Value

Customer Value

$$CV = \left(\text{Customers total perceived benefit} - \text{Customers total cost}\right)$$

Without rewriting the chapter on value visualisation, you will obviously need to ask questions to uncover the difference the solution has made. Customer Value equates to the total perceived benefit less the total cost. The key word here is perceived value, which encompasses tangible as well as intangible benefits, i.e. it includes feelings and opinion.

I'm sure your product or platform has some key deliverables and metrics that can be reported on which will provide some quick measures of the impact. For example, if you're selling a recruitment tool, you can demonstrate how the system has optimised the applicant tracking including the number of applicants, time to hire, time to start and so on.

Taking a temperature check

To uncover both emotional responses and less tangible benefits start by asking some open questions but with a purpose.

> How are you finding the service?
> What's good about what it does (or what we do)?
> What does the business think about the results it is providing?
> What value has it added?

These questions may be broad, but the answers can offer valuable insights. It's essential to recognize any underlying signals in the responses. For instance, if someone says, "Erm... yes, it's okay," you should evaluate their tone and confidence. Is their body language aligned with their words? Additionally, asking "What does the boss think?" can reveal their proximity or detachment from the situation.

Calculate, Validate and Emanate

Understanding and communicating the value your solution brings to the customer is paramount. But it's not just about understanding that value; it's about calculating it, validating it, and then emanating it to the right stakeholders.

Let's break down these three critical steps.

Calculate Quantify the Value	What is better? By how much (suggestive reasoning)? Work your Champion and coaches Document all tangible and intangible metrics
↓	
Validate Ensure the value is recognised	Who will validate the value (authority influence)? What proof do you have? Triangulation of information
↓	
Emanate Broadcast the value	Who knows about the value? Who should know about the value? How will they find out about it?

Quantifying the Value

As we already discussed utilise the conversations that were had during the sale and the handover from the sales account manager to use as the goal and targets. Also, this would / should have also been captured during the onboarding phase.

Utilise Impact Questions to uncover the various aspects on Time, Money, People, Processes and Plans (see Value Visualisation). If the client is a little unsure of the answers or numbers utilise suggestive reasoning as a tool.

Suggestive reasoning is a cognitive process where one proposes ideas or solutions based on preliminary evidence, patterns, or analogies, rather than definitive proof. It's about making educated guesses or suggestions that seem likely based on the available information. In the context of sales and customer interactions, suggestive reasoning can be used to guide clients towards a particular conclusion or action by presenting them with compelling, albeit not conclusive, arguments or scenarios.

For instance, if a salesperson knows that a similar company benefited significantly from a particular feature of their product, they might suggest that the client could experience similar benefits. While not a guarantee, it's a reasoned suggestion based on analogous evidence. In essence, suggestive reasoning is about connecting the dots in a way that seems logical and probable, even if it's not definitive. It's a powerful tool in persuasive communication, allowing one to influence decisions and perceptions based on probable outcomes or similarities.

Every sales process has a champion, someone within the client's organisation who believes in your solution, and usually is the person who drives the buying cycle to bring it into the business. Collaborate closely with them to understand and document the tangible (cost savings, efficiency gains) and intangible (employee satisfaction, brand reputation) benefits they're experiencing.

It's essential to maintain a comprehensive record of all value metrics. This documentation serves as a foundation for future discussions and can be a powerful tool in upselling or cross-selling scenarios In the Time to Grow phase. Equally, this data and insight can become sales collateral and a use case study.

Ensuring the Value is Recognised

It's not enough for you or your champion to recognise the value; it needs validation from someone with authority or influence within the client's organisation. This could be a department head, a C-suite executive, or even an external consultant.

Anecdotal evidence is a start, but hard data speaks volumes. Whether it's usage statistics, efficiency metrics, or customer feedback, gather concrete proof of the value your solution is delivering and then **triangulate the Information**. Triangulation, in the context of information gathering and validation, refers to the practice of using multiple sources or methods to collect data on the same topic. The primary purpose of triangulation is to enhance the accuracy, credibility, and validity of the information being collected.

When gathering information, relying on a single source can lead to biased or incomplete insights. By cross-referencing information from multiple sources, you can identify inconsistencies, fill in gaps, and gain a more holistic understanding of the subject at hand.

Furthermore, triangulation acts as a safeguard against misinformation. In today's digital age, where information is abundant but not always accurate, it's easy to fall prey to false or misleading data. By cross-checking facts and figures from different sources, you reduce the risk of basing decisions on erroneous information.

Most importantly, triangulation means that you don't fall foul of someone disagreeing with you, or calling out the numbers and undermining you at a later date.

In essence, triangulating information is a rigorous approach to ensure that the insights you gather are not only comprehensive but also trustworthy. It's a method that reinforces the principle that multiple perspectives and sources lead to a richer, more accurate understanding of any given topic.

Triangulate information by gathering feedback from multiple stakeholders, comparing it against industry benchmarks, and analysing it in the context of the client's specific goals and challenges.

Broadcasting the Value

Understand who's already aware of the value and, more importantly, who should be. This could range from other departments within the client's organisation to external stakeholders like investors or industry analysts.

It's not just about broadcasting the value; it's about communicating it in a way that resonates with the target audience. Tailor your message based on the stakeholder's role, priorities, and challenges.

Whether it's through formal reports, presentations, case studies, or even informal discussions, ensure that the value message permeates through multiple channels, reaching all relevant stakeholders. Bear in mind the level of reporting that you deliver, the more senior the person, the more strategic they will be. Therefore ensure you link it back to PBOs and organisational objectives, not just operational KPIs.

In essence, the journey from calculating to emanating value is a meticulous process that requires collaboration, validation, and strategic communication. By following these steps, sales teams can not only demonstrate the value they're delivering but also ensure that it's recognised, appreciated, and acted upon by the right stakeholders.

Time to Grow

Of course, as businesses grow and evolve, their needs change and throughout the QBR process one should be having regular check-ins with your customers to understand their current challenges, future plans, and any gaps that your solutions might fill. This proactive approach ensures that you're always aligned with their goals and can offer timely solutions. But it doesn't happen by chance.

As we saw earlier, QBR 1 and 2 can be focused on onboarding and capturing value, but within QBR 2, one can start to open up a deeper discovery of the business and delve more in to the client's business goals and strategies. In those conversations, the customer is not expecting the conversation to be sales-driven and will be more willing to share openly about pain points and opportunities to evolve.

QBR 3 – Time to Show

Not necessarily always the right time, but if we take the action of QBR 2 was to start a deeper discovery into the client's business, QBR 3 would be the ideal time to engage the customer in to putting the software and platform through its paces. It is a perfect time to show the customer the potential of the service and 'What's Possible'. It is time to introduce additional features, modules, or services that complement what the customer is already using.

Be careful though, this shouldn't be a hard sell. it should come from a place of genuine understanding of their needs and planting seeds around additional options or services that can help them achieve their objectives faster or more efficiently.

I repeat, this isn't about selling - it's about becoming a trusted advisor to your customers by knowledge-sharing and offering best practice guides. Consider your role as their performance manager or a high-performance coach – what could you do that will enhance their performance and maximise their efficiency? How about introducing them to other customers who have faced similar challenges, or showing they faster and better ways of utilising the tools, or demonstrating other performance-enhancing add-ons? Becoming a valuable resource you ensure that the relationship goes beyond a transactional one and you move in to a position of trust and authority.

From a commercial standpoint, establishing new ideas, planting seeds and establishing opportunities to grow the account at the Q3 stage will mean that the customer has time to build the cost of the additional upgrades into next year's budget. Those who wait till the renewal date to discuss upgrades will testify that it is hard to get them across the line as the customer has already committed the budget and therefore has a tendency to put off the upgrades with, 'let's take a look at the end of the next quarter'. In essence the customer now needs to wait and see if they can fit them into the current budget.

QBR 4 & Growth Alignment

As you can guess, QBR 4 is where you sign the customer up for the renewal. Renewal rates vary depending on whether the QBRs have delivered and you have ensured user adoption, demonstrated ROI, linked it to positive business outcomes and so on. Let's not rehash the last couple of pages and or even chapters. Suffice it to say that those companies that see high renewal rates do all the things we have discussed thus far and those that see low renewal rates wait till those 90 / 60 /30 days out to start the conversations. Having the renewal conversation, including price increases, upsells and cross-sells will become easier and not require any 'closing techniques' to make it happen.

Remember, selling subscription-based services it's not about meeting the immediate needs of your clients, that might be what enticed them to buy, but what keeps them coming back and staying as long-term customers is your ability to foresee their future requirements and aligning your solutions to cater to those evolving needs. This is the essence of growth alignment.

Every business, regardless of its size or industry, aspires for growth. As they scale, their challenges and requirements change. What worked for them when they were a start-up might not be as effective when they transition into a mid-sized company or a large enterprise. Their technological needs, user base, data management requirements, and even their customer engagement strategies might undergo significant transformations.

As a SaaS / Tech provider, understanding these growth trajectories is crucial. It's not about selling a product, it's about selling a vision. A vision where your solution seamlessly scales and evolves in tandem with your client's growth. This proactive approach not only cements your position as a trusted partner but also reduces the chances of clients looking elsewhere for solutions as they grow.

But how do you ensure this alignment? It starts with open communication and also engaging the senior stakeholders. My experience is that senior stakeholder get involved in the procurement process, ensuring that it is strategically aligned to the business needs, but once the system is purchased they are not involved after that, especially with the vendor. Making the QBR's not just about 'how is it going' and engaging with your clients to understand their growth plans, potential market expansions, and any anticipated shifts in their business model, will give you a clear picture of where they're headed and allows you to tailor your offerings accordingly and also enables Time to Show, much more valuable in the stakeholders eyes.

New technologies emerge, customer preferences shift, and market dynamics change, so also invest in R&D. By staying at the forefront of innovation and continuously refining your product, you ensure that your solutions remain relevant and competitive, ready to cater to your clients' future needs.

Lastly, foster a culture of adaptability within your team. Encourage them to think long-term and train them to anticipate market shifts and emerging trends. Equip them with the skills and knowledge to not just react to changes but to proactively address them.

In essence, growth alignment is about future-proofing. It's about ensuring that as your clients grow and evolve, you're right there with them, every step of the way, guiding, supporting, and delivering unmatched value.

"Time to Grow" is about ensuring that the value you provide to your customers is not static. It's about continuously looking for opportunities to enhance that value, ensuring that they not only remain loyal customers but also become advocates for your brand.

Customer Feedback (Double Loop Learning)

Before we move on to the next chapter, I think this could be a good time to discuss gathering customer feedback as part of the strategic direction and being customer-centric. In the 'Gathering Insights' chapter we looked at Double Loop feedback.

Including customer feedback is crucial in the double-loop learning process, especially in a sales context. Customer feedback provides direct insights into how products or services are perceived, what's working, and what needs improvement. When integrated into the double-loop feedback process, customer feedback can lead to more informed and effective revisions of underlying assumptions and strategies.

Here's how a double-loop feedback process can be incorporated when gathering customer feedback.

QBR & data capture:	Use various channels to collect feedback, such as surveys, focus groups, online reviews, direct interactions, and social media monitoring. Ensure that the feedback collection process is systematic and ongoing. Identify common themes, patterns, and pain points. Look for feedback that challenges the current assumptions or beliefs about the product, the market, or the sales process.
Single-loop Response:	Address immediate concerns raised by customers. For instance, if customers mention that the product delivery is slow, the immediate response might be to streamline the delivery process.
Double-loop Inquiry:	Dive deeper into the feedback to question foundational beliefs and assumptions: *Why do customers perceive the product in a certain way?* *Are there recurring issues that indicate a misalignment between the product and market needs?* *Is the sales team communicating the product's value proposition eff ectively?Are there unmet needs or desires that the product could address?*
Revise Assumptions:	Use the insights from customer feedback to challenge and potentially revise underlying assumptions. For example, if customers consistently mention that a feature is unnecessary, it might be worth reconsidering the product design or how it's marketed.

Adopting a customer-centric approach ensures that sales strategies are finely tuned to align with the genuine needs and desires of customers. This alignment not only fosters a sense of trust but also makes customers feel truly valued, especially when they witness their feedback translating into tangible changes. By directly engaging with customers and understanding their perspectives, businesses can significantly reduce the guesswork and assumptions that often cloud decision-making processes.

Conclusion

The power of placing the customer at the heart of every decision cannot be overstated. Through our journey in understanding the essence of Customer Centricity, we've delved deep into the importance of engaging with clients on a profound level, visualising and delivering tangible value, and aligning our growth strategies with their aspirations. Each of these facets plays a pivotal role in not just acquiring customers but nurturing and retaining them for the long haul, after all, Lifetime Value is where profitability sits.

However, while being customer-centric lays a robust foundation, it's only one piece of the puzzle. To truly dominate in a downturn and set your organisation apart in a competitive market, there's a need to elevate your strategies further. This brings us to our next force, one that encapsulates the essence of standing out and making an indelible mark: **Distinctive Dominance**.

As we transition into exploring the intricacies of Distinctive Dominance, remember the lessons of Customer Centricity. They will serve as the bedrock upon which we build strategies that not only distinguish us from the competition but position us as leaders and innovators in the SaaS realm.

4

Dd

Force 4:
Distinctive Dominance

4

Dd

Contents

Distinctive Dominance

The beauty and the pain of software and technology solutions are that new entrants continually disrupt the market and existing players constantly pivot to meet changing demands. This means establishing a firm foothold requires more than just a stellar product. It demands a distinctive dominance, i.e. a clear, compelling competitive advantage that sets a business apart and ensures its continued growth and relevance. But how can a tech business achieve this dominance?

Every business has strengths, whether it is with the compilation of features, expertise, or insights that competitors can't easily replicate. Distinctive dominance begins with a deep understanding of these strengths and leveraging them to create a strong value proposition. It's about knowing what sets you apart and communicating that difference compellingly to your target audience. It is a lot more than a competitive advantage, especially since competitive advantage isn't just in the product, it's the people surrounding it. Equipping your sales and customer success teams with the right tools, insights, and strategies ensures they can effectively communicate your unique value proposition, overcome objections, and foster lasting client relationships. It's about creating a culture of excellence and a shared vision of success.

Distinctive dominance is also more than the ability to acquire new clients, it is about nurturing existing ones. In a slower economy, where new opportunities might be scarce, focusing on expanding and deepening relationships with current clients becomes paramount. This means identifying opportunities for upselling, cross-selling, and ensuring that clients derive maximum value from your product, leading to increased loyalty and advocacy.

Strategic positioning is also a key factor. It's about identifying the right niches, understanding market dynamics, and strategically placing your product to address specific pain points or gaps. Distinctive dominance involves not just being another player in the market but being the go-to solution for specific challenges or industries.

In this section, Force 4: Distinctive Dominance, we'll explore the intricacies of achieving distinctive dominance and delve into how businesses can carve out their unique space, ensuring they thrive, even in challenging economic conditions.

Enhancing Competitive Advantage

As quickly as a new product hits the marketplace, you will see replication and new entrants arrive shortly thereafter. Especially with the fast acceleration of AI, a new product turns up and suddenly the market is saturated with options and competition is fierce.

Understanding and articulating your competitive advantage is essential for survival. This understanding forms the bedrock upon which all your sales and marketing strategies are built. It's what makes your product or service stand out in a crowded marketplace.

Your competitive advantage might stem from a variety of sources: perhaps it's your product's unique functionality, your company's industry expertise, or the innovative use of technology that others have yet to leverage. It could also be the exceptional customer service you provide, the community you've built around your product, or the way you've integrated feedback into your development cycle to ensure your product continually evolves with your customers' needs.

What is Competitive Advantage

In essence, competitive advantage is the leverage a business has over its competitors, allowing it to generate greater sales or margins and retain more customers. It's what makes an entity's goods or services superior to all other choices. While the concept is simple, the practice of cultivating a competitive advantage can be complex and multifaceted.

Michael E. Porter, a professor at Harvard Business School and a leading authority on competitive strategy, defines competitive advantage as the ability to perform activities differently or to perform different activities than rivals. This advantage comes from attributes that allow an organization to outperform its competition, such as access to natural resources, highly skilled labour, geographic location, high entry barriers, and access to new technology.

To truly understand your competitive advantage, you must look inward and outward. Internally, this means having a clear grasp of your product's strengths and how these translate into benefits for your customers. Externally, it involves a thorough analysis of the market and your competitors. What are they offering, and where do they fall short? Where are the gaps that your product can fill? This is where the insights from Force 2, Insight Agility, become invaluable. By harnessing data and feedback, you can pinpoint exactly where your product stands out.

Implementing Competitive Advantage

To implement a competitive advantage, a company must first understand its distinctive value proposition. Remember, your products or services might not in itself be unique, but how you compile them, or how you do them better than everyone else, makes them distinctively different and a Distinctive Selling Point, a DSP rather than a USP. You DSP must be communicated effectively, ensuring that all team members are aligned with the company's strategic positioning. This involves training and development programs that help employees understand not only what sets the company apart but also how to leverage these differences in every customer interaction.

Once you've identified your competitive advantage, the next step is to ensure that it is communicated effectively. This is where the lessons from Force 1, Disruptive Mindset, come into play. It's not enough to have a superior product or service; your potential customers need to understand why it's superior and how it will make a difference in their lives. This messaging must be clear, compelling, and consistent across all your marketing and sales channels.

In Seth Godin's "The Purple Cow," the central theme of creating remarkable products is extended to the realm of selling services, especially in the technology and affiliated sectors. Godin's metaphor of the Purple Cow emphasizes not just the uniqueness of a product, but also the distinctive selling points (DSPs) that set a service apart in a crowded market. For tech and SaaS companies, this means developing and highlighting features or benefits that are not only unique but are also directly aligned with the customers' needs and pain points.

DSPs could range from offering unparalleled customer support, innovative pricing models, superior usability, to integration capabilities that no other service provides. The essence of Godin's argument is that for a service to be remarkable, it must offer something that not only captures attention but also delivers substantial value in a way that competitors do not. This requires a deep understanding of the target market, a commitment to innovation, and the agility to adapt to changing customer demands, sound familiar.

For tech and SaaS companies, marketing a service with distinctive selling points involves demonstrating how these DSPs solve specific problems or enhance efficiency in ways that are tangible and meaningful to the customer. It's about creating a service so compelling that its users naturally become its promoters, sharing their positive experiences and the unique benefits they've gained. In this way, a service can transcend being merely a tool or a platform as it becomes an indispensable solution that clients cannot imagine doing without. This is the power of the Purple Cow, transforming the exceptional into the essential, through clear, innovative DSPs that meet and exceed customer expectations.

Empowering your team to communicate this advantage is crucial. They should be well-versed in the Distinctive Selling Points of your product and confident in articulating them. This is where continuous learning and development, a key component of Force 3, Client Centricity, becomes critical. Your team's ability to convey your competitive advantage in a way that resonates with clients will set the stage for deeper engagement and long-term loyalty.

Leveraging Competitive Advantage for Distinctive Dominance

We can see that competitive advantage is the linchpin for distinctive dominance. It's the value proposition that differentiates a product from its competitors. But identifying your competitive advantage is just the first step, the real challenge lies in leveraging it effectively to achieve market dominance.

Understanding and Articulating Your DSP

Your DSP is the essence of your competitive advantage. The first step is to understand this DSP in its entirety and then articulate it in a way that resonates with your target audience. Take, for example, Salesforce's approach: they didn't just offer a cloud-based CRM; they created an adaptable ecosystem that allowed for unparalleled customization. This adaptability became their competitive edge, their DSP that set them apart. Other, and many other companies offer CRM systems and SalesForce were certainly not the first player or early market entrance, but is now the market leader.

Innovation keeps your competitive advantage sharp. It's not enough to rest on the laurels of current features or services. Continuous improvement and adaptation to the changing market needs are essential. Look at how Slack maintains its dominance by continuously adding integrations and features that enhance user experience, staying ahead of potential competitors, and Zoom for how it leveraged its simplicity and reliability to provide a seamless experience that retained user loyalty even as numerous alternatives flooded the market during the pandemic.

Your competitive advantage should manifest in every aspect of the customer experience. This means that every interaction, from the initial website visit to ongoing post-sale support, should reinforce your DSPs.

Incorporating Real-World Success Stories into Your Sales Strategy

The narrative you craft is as crucial as the product you're selling. To truly captivate your prospects and illustrate the unique value of your offering, you need to weave in real-world success stories that resonate on a personal level. These stories should chart a journey that your prospects can see themselves embarking on, one that takes them from a familiar challenge to a solution, culminating in a transformative outcome.

Developing in-depth case studies of your most successful clients is essential. These narratives should delve into the specifics—how your product's unique features were instrumental in overcoming their challenges and achieving their goals. It's about painting a picture so vivid that your prospects can't help but see their own potential success reflected in it.

Complement these stories with insights from industry leaders who have consistently stayed ahead of the curve. Their perspectives on navigating market trends, understanding customer needs, and driving innovation can serve as a guiding star for leveraging your competitive advantage.

And let's not forget the power of data. Quantifiable results can turn a good story into an undeniable one. Showcasing how your product has not just met but exceeded expectations, with clear metrics of improved efficiency, profitability, or customer satisfaction, can be the tipping point for a prospect on the fence.

By integrating these elements into your sales conversations, you're not just selling a product, you're offering a proven path to success. It's about building trust through credibility and helping your prospects envision the success that's within their reach with your solution.

Actionable Strategies

It's not enough to simply have a competitive advantage, or be the better product, you must wield it effectively in the marketplace. The tech space is awash with technologies that were by far superior to others on the market but lost out due to poor strategy execution. Here are strategies you can implement to ensure your competitive edge is not just understood internally but is also the driving force of your distinctive dominance:

Competitor Analysis:	Stay informed about your competitors. Regularly analyse their offerings, strengths, and weaknesses. This knowledge enables you to confidently position your product's distinctive selling proposition (DSP) against competitors, highlighting why your solution is the superior choice.
Customer Feedback Loops:	Create robust channels for customer feedback. This direct line to customer experiences is invaluable. It informs product development, ensuring your DSP continues to solve real-world problems and marketing strategies, keeping your messaging relevant and impactful.
Targeted Marketing:	Your marketing efforts should be laser-focused on spotlighting your competitive advantage or Purple Cow. Develop narratives that go beyond listing features; tell the story of the problems your product solves. Make it relatable and compelling, so your target audience can see the tangible benefits of choosing your solution over others.

By integrating these strategies into your operations, you can ensure that your competitive advantage is not just a concept but a tangible asset that drives your sales and cements your position as a leader in the market.

Distinctive dominance is about more than just having a competitive advantage, it's about leveraging that advantage in a way that resonates with customers and constantly evolves with the market. By understanding, articulating, and innovating on your DSP, you can create a unique customer experience that not only attracts but retains a loyal customer base.

Success Blueprint

Let me introduce the Success Blueprint. OK, sounds simple but it is something a little more special than it seems. For you and I, it is a strategic imperative to demonstrate distinctive dominance and to the mere observer it may appear simple, but let me assure you, the bulk of your competitors cannot do it and if they do, they do not do it correctly. The Blueprint is a roadmap that guides customers through the complexities of implementing your product, ensuring they not only understand its features but also how to leverage them for maximum impact. The blueprint is a testament to your commitment to their success and a powerful tool for establishing your distinctive dominance in the market.

What is the Blueprint

A Success Blueprint is a comprehensive framework that outlines the journey a customer will take from initial onboarding to full-scale utilisation, optimisation and beyond. It's not a training plan, it is a strategic plan that encompasses all aspects of the customer experience, tailored to ensure that each user not only achieves their goals with your product but also recognizes and can articulate the value it adds to their business.

But don't think of it as a document. It's a strategic tool that positions your company as a partner in your customer's success. By providing a clear, actionable plan for leveraging your product to achieve business goals, you're demonstrating a level of commitment and foresight that goes beyond the typical vendor-customer relationship. This approach not only enhances customer satisfaction and loyalty but also establishes your company as a leader in the market, one that truly understands and is invested in the success of its customers, not invested in simply getting them to use your technology.

At its core, a Success Blueprint is about intention. It's a deliberate, thought-out plan that anticipates the customer's needs, objectives, and potential challenges. It's not a one-size-fits-all checklist but a dynamic, living document that adapts to the customer's evolving requirements.

Crafting the Components of a Success Blueprint

Remember this is a strategic framework that guides customers through the journey of maximizing the value from your platform. It's a tailored plan that aligns with the customer's business objectives, providing a clear path to success and ensuring they fully leverage the product's capabilities.

The component parts of the blueprint should demonstrate to the customer how they will be set up for success. It should include the following elements:

- Onboarding
- Milestones and Metrics
- Customer Success
- Resource Allocation
- Personalised Approach

Onboarding

The first element is the onboarding process and is where the customer forms their first impressions of your product and its potential impact on their business. A well-structured onboarding experience is crucial, as it sets the tone for the customer relationship. Authors like Lincoln Murphy have emphasized the significance of onboarding, noting that a customer's initial experience with a product can significantly influence their long-term success and satisfaction.

In the Blueprint it should be comprehensive, easy to digest, and personalized to address the specific needs and goals of the customer. All too often, a lot of emphasis on the sale's rollout is simply placed on the onboarding and driving user adoption aspects of the rollout. These things are important to ensure that the renewal happens, but they are not the deciding factor if the system provides benefit.

An example of this was when I was working with an online legal library provider. Their client base incorporated law firms of all different sizes and of course they needed to drive engagement and adoption to ensure the organisation received value from the service. One would argue that if their client had 1500 lawyers, training them on how to use the platform was imperative to driving user adoption and ensuring renewals. The truth is that the provider doesn't need 1500 lawyers to adopt and use the system, especially when they have librarians (now known as knowledge managers) and legal researchers who do the legal searches and pull the various laws and citations for the lawyers. The true value of onboarding is gaining buy-in from the organisation to utilise the data and to ensure the researchers are up to speed as soon as possible and utilise the functionality as quickly as possible. The client utilised a value-based pricing model, which meant that 1500 lawyers received the benefit of the system, even though only 10% may log in and access the platform.

Milestones and Metrics

Identifying and setting clear milestones and metrics is essential for tracking progress and ensuring alignment with the customer's business goals. These KPIs act as signposts along the customer's journey, providing tangible evidence of the product's value. In "The Lean Startup," Eric Ries discusses the importance of actionable metrics in driving continuous improvement and growth, a principle that applies equally to the customer's journey with any SaaS or tech-based product.

In essence, he discusses that you need to make sure you plot when and how you will track, measure and report on the impact, not just what you are going to track. Building this into the plan, provides confidence in different stakeholders that this is a strategic implementation, not a product sale. We discussed in Force 3, the concept of 'Time to Value', and focusing on the idea of spending the first quarter or two to not only drive 'Time to Live', I.e. getting the customer onboarded, and then focusing on 'Time to Value' to enable the customer to see and feel they are receiving value from the solution.

Milestones and metrics are also important to try and envision for a longer term, not just for Q1 or H1 or Year 1. The success blueprint should force you to consider future benefits not just what it can do right now for the client. David Allen's groundbreaking work on productivity, epitomized in his book "Getting Things Done" (GTD), has offered many individuals and organizations, including several of my clients, a structured framework to enhance efficiency and achieve their goals. The reason I am sharing this here is that a fundamental component of Allen's methodology is the Natural Planning Model, which mirrors the way our minds naturally plan and execute tasks. Without going into depth about the whole model, The first two steps of this model, defining the purpose and visioning outcomes, are critical for setting a strong foundation for any project.

Defining the purpose serves as the cornerstone of the GTD approach. This step is about gaining clarity on why a project is worth undertaking. Allen emphasizes that understanding the underlying reason for a project not only provides direction but also serves as a source of motivation and alignment. It's about asking the fundamental question, "Why is this important?" This inquiry helps in focusing efforts on what truly matters, ensuring that the subsequent actions are meaningful and aligned with broader goals or values.

Following the definition of purpose, the next step, visioning outcomes, invites one to engage in a process of 'envisioning wild success'. Allen encourages a bold and unrestricted approach to this process, advocating for a creative and expansive mindset. Envisioning the best possible outcome involves imagining the project's completion in vivid detail, considering the highest level of success achievable. This step is not just about setting goals but about stretching the imagination beyond conventional limits to inspire ambition and innovation. By picturing the most successful scenario, individuals can reverse-engineer the path to achievement, identifying specific milestones and metrics that will guide their progress.

Together, these two steps in Allen's Natural Planning Model, defining the purpose and visioning outcomes, lay a robust foundation for a successful implementation. They encapsulate the essence of creating a success blueprint, where clear intentions and ambitious visions pave the way for actionable steps towards realisation. Incorporating these principles into your blueprint for success not only aligns with Allen's philosophy but also enriches the approach with a structured yet flexible framework that is adaptable to a wide range of goals and projects.

Customer Success & Resource Allocation

An often-underplayed differentiator in many sales scenarios is the role of trainers, system implementers/integrators, and customer success managers. I have seen so many salespeople tell the customer that they get a dedicated customer success manager, and or trainers, etc., but they do not articulate the value that this brings. Allocating the right resources is about more than just providing access to tools and materials. It's about ensuring customers have the support they need when they need it, which might include dedicated customer success managers but also comprehensive knowledge bases and/or community forums.

The goal is to create an environment where customers have easy access to the resources that will help them succeed. You must demonstrate within the Blueprint the resource allocation that is dedicated to enabling the implementation to be successful. Again, this will reinforce the confidence in the solution the customer is buying.

Expanding on this, a well-thought-out customer success strategy is holistic, encompassing not only the immediate post-sale period but the entire lifecycle of the customer's engagement with the product. It's about mapping out and investing in a journey that brings continual value to the customer, thereby fostering a relationship that encourages growth, retention, and loyalty.

To truly articulate the value of resources like customer success managers, you must highlight their role in pre-emptively addressing potential issues, facilitating smoother onboarding processes, and acting as advocates for the customer within the company. This involves setting clear expectations, providing regular progress check-ins, and maintaining a dialogue that goes beyond mere troubleshooting. It's about creating a partnership where the customer not only feels supported but empowered. Again, as we saw in Force 3, Customer Centricity, showing the concept of the QBR process, and the reasons behind it, would also engage senior stakeholders and drive them to attend the QBR meetings.

In terms of resource allocation, emphasize the scalability and adaptability of support structures. For instance, the implementation of AI-driven chatbots for 24/7 query resolution or the use of data analytics to personalize the customer experience can significantly enhance efficiency and satisfaction. Discuss the investment in continuous training for customer-facing teams to ensure they are experts not only in the product but also in communication and problem-solving skills.

Finally, make a case for the value of community building. Developing a platform where customers can interact, share best practices, and even co-create solutions can lead to innovation and enhanced product loyalty, I am going to talk more about this later, but this communal aspect often becomes a fertile ground for advocacy and organic growth. By showing a commitment to a comprehensive, customer-centric success blueprint, businesses can differentiate themselves in a competitive market where customer experience is paramount.

Personalised Approach

A one-size-fits-all approach doesn't work in showing customers that they are important and that this is a partnership approach. Customisation is key to addressing the unique challenges and objectives of different customer segments. This tailored approach ensures that the strategies and resources provided are relevant and effective for each segment, ultimately leading to higher satisfaction and better outcomes.

With this in mind, you may consider creating the Blueprint as a piece of sales collateral for the team to utilise in presentations and pitches, which is a great idea, but make sure it is customised to the client market segment, thus reducing people's feeling it is not about them. Demonstrate thought leadership and segment expertise, helping the customer realise your organisation is the subject matter expert, but also aiding them to feel they are a little unique and customised for their particular requirements.

Shep Hyken's book 'The Cult Customer', reinforces the idea of creating such a great experience that the customers become evangelists for the service, and therefore the personalisation of the success blueprint should go beyond the mere adaptation of materials. It should inform the entire customer journey, integrating data-driven insights to tailor the experience meticulously. From the initial stages of onboarding, where individual learning styles and preferences dictate the training methods employed, to the ongoing support structure, which adjusts in real-time to the customer's evolving needs, personalisation isn't nice to have, it is a must have.

Effective personalisation considers the client's industry-specific regulatory landscape, competitive pressures, and internal company culture, ensuring the solutions provided resonate with their environment. For example, the Blueprint could include industry-specific case studies and workflow customisations that showcase an understanding of the client's unique challenges and opportunities.

Lastly, weave in how personalisation in resource allocation, as previously discussed, can lead to a deeper engagement. For instance, a customer in the healthcare sector would benefit from success managers who are well-versed in healthcare compliance and data security, while a customer in retail might value expertise in e-commerce integration and customer data analytics. By aligning, or highlighting, the resource expertise with the customer's industry, the Blueprint becomes not just a sales tool, but a strategic guide tailored to ensure the customer's success in the most personal way possible.

In summary, the personalised success blueprint should not only be customised in appearance but should embody a strategy that is inherently adaptable, responsive, and reflective of each customer's unique path to success.

Feedback Loops and Continuous Improvement

Integrating feedback mechanisms into the implementation process is not merely a supportive measure, it's a strategic component of the success blueprint that facilitates dynamic personalisation. This adaptation evolves with customer input, distinguishing our approach in a competitive marketplace. By instituting an iterative process that is deeply embedded in the Agile methodology, we ensure that our solutions remain in lockstep with the customer's shifting needs. It's a practice that not only elevates the customer experience but also serves as a testament to our unwavering dedication to continual enhancement and cooperative partnership.

Such a mechanism becomes a distinctive competitive advantage when highlighted in the Quarterly Business Review (QBR) process and showcased as a driver for ongoing product development. This degree of responsiveness signals to the customer that their feedback is not just heard but is instrumental in shaping the evolution of the product, reinforcing their role as a valued collaborator.

Embedding a culture of 'customer listening' across every facet of the organisation ensures that feedback informs all areas of customer interaction, forging a unified, customer-centric approach in decision-making. This practice is crucial for maintaining a competitive edge and turns the success blueprint into a living document that grows with the customer and the organisation.

By aligning the feedback loop with continuous learning and development, we leverage customer insights as a means to refine our internal processes. These insights become real-world case studies, enhancing the collective knowledge within the organisation and, in turn, informing the success blueprint. It's this cycle of personalised improvement and shared advancement that affords us a unique position in the market, where our commitment to the customer's success becomes our most significant competitive advantage.

Scalability and Growth

A robust Success Blueprint is prophetic in its design, envisioning a future where the customer's success is intertwined with your product's scalability. In the fabric of your blueprint, you should weave a narrative of growth that reflects the aspirations and ambitions of your clients. This is not a mere augmentation of capacity or volume. It is a thoughtful expansion of capabilities, aligning with the customer's evolving business landscape.

Try to foresee your clients not just as they are but as they aim to be, larger, more influential, and more interconnected. The blueprint should present an elastic product, one that stretches to meet the demands of increased workloads, broader geographical footprints, and more complex business processes. Infuse your offering with intelligent algorithms, modular features, and cloud scalability that anticipate the growth trajectories of the client, thus ensuring the product and services are not just a tool for today but an engine driving the successes of tomorrow.

Top and Tail

The commencement of a success blueprint is a strategic statement. It should set the tone by demonstrating an intrinsic understanding of the customer's overarching business strategy and how the product fits within it. Here, the blueprint must illustrate that the product serves as a catalyst in the customer's pursuit of their strategic goals, transforming it from a functional tool to an indispensable strategic resource. This part of the blueprint anchors the product's features and services to the customer's business objectives, ensuring that each element is purpose-built to support and enhance the customer's strategic journey.

The heart of the blueprint is where strategy is transformed into action. It is here that the document should delineate a step-by-step action plan, offering a detailed guide for translating high-level strategies into tangible outcomes. This should not only provide clarity and direction but also serve as a barometer against which the customer can measure success. Each step, each milestone, is a testament to the product's capability to turn vision into reality.

In its concluding section, the blueprint should circle back to the promises made at its inception, demonstrating how the product has been, and will continue to be, a partner in the customer's success story. This part of the document should serve as a reassurance of ongoing support, a reflection of achievements to date, and a pledge of alignment with future ambitions. It's an affirmation of the enduring partnership and a celebration of the strategic triumphs facilitated by the product.

Consider linking back to the Positive Business Outcomes (PBOs) that we have discussed in detail earlier in the book. If you have uncovered them in the discovery, sold them during the value proposition articulation, then building them into the success blueprint demonstrates the commitment to deliver them, not just using them to sell the solution.

Pre and Post Sale Tool

The Success Blueprint is typically used to describe what happens post-sale and is an integral part of the customer success strategy. It serves as a roadmap for customers, outlining the steps they will take after purchasing the product to achieve their desired outcomes. The blueprint is designed to ensure that customers not only understand the features and functionalities of the product but also how to use them effectively to meet their specific business goals.

In the sales process, the Success Blueprint can be a powerful tool for demonstrating commitment to potential customers. It shows that the company is not just interested in making a sale, but is also invested in the customer's long-term success. By presenting a clear plan for how the product will continue to deliver value, the sales team can differentiate their offering from competitors and build trust with prospects.

Here's how the Success Blueprint can be leveraged during the sales process:

Building Confidence:	By discussing the post-sale support and the Success Blueprint during the sales process, sales representatives can reassure prospects about the level of support they will receive. This can help build confidence in the decision to purchase.
Demonstrating Value:	A well-articulated Success Blueprint helps to demonstrate the ongoing value the customer will receive from the product, which can be a decisive factor in the sales process.
Reducing Perceived Risk:	For many customers, especially in B2B sales, the perceived risk of implementing a new solution can be a significant barrier. A Success Blueprint can help mitigate this by showing a clear path to achieving a return on their investment.
Facilitating Decision Making:	By providing a vision of the future relationship and the steps towards achieving success with the product, the Success Blueprint can facilitate the decision-making process for the customer.
Customisation / Personalisation:	Tailoring the Success Blueprint to the specific needs and goals of each prospect can demonstrate the company's commitment to personalization and customer-centricity.

In essence, while the Success Blueprint is primarily a post-sale tool, its implications during the sales process are profound. It not only sets the stage for a successful customer relationship but also serves as a differentiator and trust-builder during the sales cycle.

Utilising existing customer success blueprints with prospects will demonstrate your commitment to success and acts as a form of Social Proof that you deliver on your promises. It will provide confidence and demonstrate your position as a dominant market player, no matter what size your organisation is.

Building Brand Advocacy

Brand advocacy emerges as a pivotal force in carving out a distinctive dominance. It's the intangible asset that can propel a company from being a mere choice among many to become an indispensable partner for its customers. But cultivating this loyalty is no accident, it's a deliberate strategy that intertwines the fabric of a brand with the success of its users.

Brand advocacy is the culmination of consistent positive experiences, trust, and the perceived value that customers associate with a brand. It's what transforms satisfied customers into brand advocates who not only renew their subscriptions year after year but also become vocal champions of the product in their networks. This advocacy is invaluable, especially in a recurring revenue model where word-of-mouth can significantly amplify growth and market penetration.

Before we dig deeper, I want to address the often interchangeable words of loyalty and advocacy, because they surely mean the same thing, right? Well for some people it does but there is a difference. I have seen all too often that customers/users may be happy with the product and its operation, but then the product gets replaced by something else.

Loyalty and advocacy, particularly in tech, are related but have distinct concepts that reflect different levels of customer engagement and satisfaction.

Loyalty refers to customers' commitment to a product or brand over time. In software, loyal customers are those who continue to use a product, often over several iterations or versions. They may do so for a variety of reasons, such as convenience, cost, features, or simply because they're resistant to change. However, loyalty can sometimes be passive. It might not always be based on the highest levels of satisfaction but rather on a perception that the software is "good enough," barriers to exit, or the absence of better alternatives.

Advocacy, on the other hand, is a stronger endorsement. It occurs when customers are so satisfied and enthusiastic about a product that they actively promote it to others. In the software world, advocates don't just renew their subscriptions or continue to use the service themselves, they become de facto marketers, recommending the product to others, writing positive reviews, sharing their experiences on social media, or even creating user-generated content that helps to bring in new customers. Advocacy implies a high level of satisfaction and a belief that the product offers superior value or quality.

Customers may remain loyal to a software product without advocating for it. They might be satisfied with the product's performance but not to the extent that they would endorse it to others. This can happen due to a variety of factors:

Competitive Market:	Even satisfied customers might switch if a competitor offers a new feature or better pricing. The software market is highly dynamic, and brand loyalty can be challenged by fast-paced innovation.
Changing Needs:	A customer's needs may evolve, leading them to seek out different solutions. Even if they were happy with a product, it might no longer serve their changing business model, scale, or objectives.
Inertia:	Some customers continue using a product out of habit or because the cost/effort of switching is perceived to be too high, rather than out of genuine satisfaction.
Lack of Emotional Connection:	For advocacy to occur, often there needs to be an emotional connection or alignment with the brand's values or identity, which might be missing even if the product is functionally satisfactory.
Market Influences:	Sometimes decisions to switch software are driven by trends, third-party endorsements, or the broader market movement rather than by direct dissatisfaction with a product.

For a company, fostering loyalty is valuable, but cultivating advocacy can have a more significant impact on growth and market share. It suggests not only meeting basic customer expectations but exceeding them and forging an emotional or value-driven connection with the user base.

Creating a following and advocacy requires more than just a great product, it demands a holistic approach that touches every aspect of the customer journey. From the initial onboarding to ongoing support, from community engagement to personalised interactions, every touchpoint is an opportunity to deepen the customer's commitment to the brand. It's about creating a sense of belonging, where customers feel part of a larger narrative, one that resonates with their own aspirations and challenges.

In this chapter, we will explore the multifaceted strategies that companies can employ to build robust brand loyalty framework and also drive advocacy. We'll delve into the psychology behind loyalty, the tactics to foster a community, the incentives that encourage advocacy, and the consistent engagement that keeps a brand relevant. We'll also examine how personalisation, quality, feedback loops, and emotional connections can turn customers into fans.

As we navigate through these strategies, remember that advocacy is not a static achievement but a dynamic relationship. It's a continuous dialogue between a brand and its customers, evolving with the market and the customers' growing needs. By prioritising brand advocacy, businesses can secure a formidable position in the market, one that not only withstands the challenges of economic downturns but also thrives amidst them.

Community Creation

The creation of a community around a product or a particular field is akin to building a home where customers can gather, share, and grow together. It's about fostering an environment where users don't just come for a service but for the experience and camaraderie that comes with it. A strong community acts as a support system, a place for inspiration, and a breeding ground for innovation.

Benefits of a community:

Shared Experiences	When customers interact within a community, they exchange more than just tips and tricks; they share experiences. These shared experiences become stories that bind the community together, creating a collective identity that is intrinsically linked to the brand. It's these stories that often become the most compelling testimonials, showcasing the real-world impact of the technology.
Facilitating Connections	A community should be a resource-rich environment where learning is continuous and support is readily available. Whether it's through user groups, forums, or events, the goal is to create spaces where customers can connect with peers facing similar challenges. This not only enhances the value they get from the product but also reinforces their decision to choose and stay with your brand.
Nurturing Brand Advocates	Within every community, there are potential brand advocates—customers who are so satisfied with their experience that they're willing to share it with others. By recognizing and empowering these individuals, a company can turn them into powerful allies. These advocates can help onboard new customers, provide valuable feedback, and spread positive word-of-mouth.

Who Builds the Community?

The responsibility of community building typically falls under the purview of marketing, but it's a cross-functional effort. While marketing might lead the charge in terms of strategy and communication, product teams, customer success, and even sales can play pivotal roles in fostering community engagement. The key is to have a unified approach where every department understands the value of the community and contributes to its growth. I have seen some amazing communities be developed by salespeople, especially in market segments, verticals or regions, where they start to bring their own customers together and therefore promoting themselves as a subject matter expert or at least a conduit for facilitating the conversation.

Building a community is not a one-off project, it's a long-term investment in the social infrastructure of your brand. It requires commitment, resources, and a genuine desire to see your customers succeed. When done right, it can transform customers into a loyal tribe that not only believes in your product but also contributes to its continuous improvement and success.

Strategies for Building a Community

In today's digital age, technology plays a crucial role in community building. From online forums to virtual events, the tools used to engage with customers must be intuitive, accessible, and conducive to interaction. Investing in the right technology can make the difference between a passive user base and an active, engaged community. With that in mind to build a community, here are 6 top tips for launching one:

Identify the Purpose and Audience: Start by defining the purpose of your community. Is it to provide support, gather feedback, or something else? Knowing your audience and their needs will shape the community's direction.

Choose the Right Platform: Whether it's a dedicated forum on your website, a Slack channel, or a group on a social media platform such as LinkedIn, choose a platform that your customers are comfortable with and that supports the kind of interactions you want to encourage.

Create Engaging Content: Regularly post content that is valuable to your community. This could be tips on using your product, industry insights, or customer success stories. The content should encourage discussion and sharing.

Encourage Interaction: Pose questions, create polls, and start discussions to encourage active participation. Recognise and reward the most active members to incentivise engagement.

Host Events: Organize webinars, Q&A sessions with product experts, or virtual meetups to bring the community together. These events can be pivotal in strengthening the community bonds.

Provide Exclusive Benefits: Offer early access to new features, exclusive content, or special discounts to community members. This not only adds value to the membership but also creates a sense of exclusivity and privilege.

As we cultivate a sense of exclusivity and privilege within our community by offering exclusive benefits, we lay the groundwork for a powerful transition into advocacy. I can cite quite a few organisations that are amazing at driving advocacy including Apple, Adobe, GitHub and others but the example I want to present is Salesforce to provide some examples of how to expand your communities in different directions.

Salesforce.com has been adept at creating communities and nurturing brand advocacy, focusing on its users and developers. Their approach is centred around the idea of creating a shared space where users can engage, learn, and contribute.

Here's a look at how Salesforce has built its communities to bolster brand advocacy:

Trailhead: Salesforce's Trailhead is an interactive, gamified online learning platform designed to teach people how to use Salesforce. It is a cornerstone of their community-building efforts, as it allows users to learn at their own pace, earn badges, and connect with others. Trailhead fosters a sense of accomplishment and community as users share their progress and help each other learn.

Salesforce Community Cloud (now Experience Cloud): This is a platform that allows companies to create their own branded online communities. It enables direct interaction between customers, partners, and employees. Users can exchange ideas, find answers to their questions, and provide product feedback, which Salesforce can use to improve its offerings.

Salesforce Events - Dreamforce and TrailheaDX: Salesforce hosts Dreamforce, one of the largest tech conferences in the world, which brings together the global Salesforce community for learning, fun, community building, and philanthropy. They also host TrailheaDX, which is a developer conference. Both events are key for community engagement, providing opportunities for learning, networking, and sharing experiences.

MVP Program: Salesforce's MVP Program recognizes exceptional community members for their leadership, knowledge, and ongoing contributions to the community. MVPs are brand advocates who help others in the Salesforce ecosystem, sharing their expertise and experiences.

User Groups: Salesforce supports and promotes user groups around the world, allowing users to meet locally to discuss Salesforce products and share experiences. These user groups enable customers to connect with peers in their own cities and industries.

IdeaExchange: The Salesforce IdeaExchange is a forum where users can suggest features and improvements to Salesforce products. Other users can vote on these ideas, and Salesforce takes these suggestions seriously, often implementing them into their products. This gives users a voice in the product's development, fostering a strong sense of ownership and community.

AppExchange: This is a marketplace for third-party applications that integrate with Salesforce. It's not only a platform for users to find useful additions to their Salesforce suite but also a community where developers can showcase their products and users can leave reviews and feedback, creating a dynamic ecosystem of innovation and support.

Salesforce Philanthropy: The company's 1-1-1 model of philanthropy, which contributes one percent of the company's equity, one percent of its employees' time, and one percent of its product to the community, also helps build a strong sense of community and shared purpose.

Through these and other initiatives, Salesforce.com has managed to create a vibrant community that extends beyond mere product usage to include shared learning, collaboration, and co-creation, all of which are central to fostering brand advocacy.

People feel exceedingly proud to be part of these groups. They not only enhance the user experience but also prime our most engaged customers to become champions of our brand.

Turning Customers into Champions

This natural progression leads us to the next critical phase in driving advocacy, fostering advocacy incentives. Advocacy incentives are the catalysts that transform satisfied customers into vocal ambassadors. By recognizing and rewarding the contributions of our community members, we can encourage them to share their positive experiences with a wider audience, extending the reach of our brand and solidifying their loyalty. Let's explore how we can effectively implement advocacy incentives to amplify your brand's presence and create a self-sustaining cycle of loyalty, advocacy and growth.

Customer loyalty is gold and advocacy incentives serve as a strategic tool to turn your users into brand champions. These incentives are designed to reward customers who actively promote your product, whether through word-of-mouth, social media, or case studies. The goal is to create a win-win scenario where customers feel appreciated for their endorsements, and your brand benefits from authentic, peer-driven marketing. Not only that, people trust the opinions of those they know and respect far more than any advertisement.

By creating a structured advocacy incentive program, you can harness this power. Offer rewards such as discounts, exclusive features, or early access to new releases to customers who refer new business or share their positive experiences with your product.

Recognition and Rewards

Recognition is a key element of any advocacy program. Publicly acknowledging your most active advocates not only rewards them but also encourages others to follow suit. This can be done through leaderboards, shoutouts in newsletters, or featuring them in case studies. Rewards can range from tangible benefits like gift cards or swag to intangible ones like VIP status or access to exclusive events.

Remember that different people are motivated in different ways. Arthur Carmazzi, in his book Architects of Extraordinary Team Culture, defined eight emotional drivers that help answer why people do what they do, and what their drivers are for doing it. He brought them into eight key aspects:

Belonging	a sense of belonging, either with people or with a cause
Security	that feeling of being safe and in control
Diversity	doing different things and a mix of variety in your life
Challenge	personal development, learning, stepping out of the comfort zone
Recognition	being recognised for your achievements and for your virtues
Achievement	to finish things and progress forward
Excellence	self-satisfaction and pride in the things you do
Contribution	feeling of contributing and making a difference

In his book he points out that not all drivers are equal, and each person will have primary drivers and their level of commitment to certain tasks and projects and the mix of these drivers will have a direct impact on the person's motivation. From these

Knowing your customers' emotional drivers enables you to be selective in your engagements and look for ways to trigger these emotions through your correspondence, value propositions and negotiations.

Here's some examples of emotional drivers and triggers:

Innovation & change They interested in solutions that are new, creative and innovative	vs	**Traditional & conservative** Interested in solutions that are tried and tested, follow a well-trodden path.
Aspirational Aspiring to move up the career ladder or they may be new into an organisation and want to make their mark	vs	**Comfortable** More comfortable and stable in their role and not motivated by what others think
Leading the business Taking decisions and being seen as someone who makes things happen	vs	**Consensus driven** Being inclusive in decision making and gaining team consensus is a real motivator
Groundbreaking Groundbreaking inventions and brand-new ways of working, trail-blazer	vs	**Conventional** Inspired by bringing in best practice, proven to work in their industry
Subject matter expert Burning desire to be the best, or an authority on the subject matter, set the standard for others	vs	**Breadth of influence** Focus on broad coverage and influence across the business

It is not that these triggers are individual ones, it is more of a combination of some of the above, e.g. the person could be aspirational and keen to move up the org chart, wants to be seen to drive the business forward and be an instigator of change. Understanding your client's motivations and emotional triggers can help you identify which aspects of the reward and recognition would motivate them and incentivise them to become advocates.

Remember the ultimate aim of advocacy incentives is to create a self-sustaining cycle of loyalty and growth. Satisfied customers become advocates, their endorsements bring in new customers, and the cycle repeats. This not only helps in scaling your customer base but also in building a strong, loyal community around your brand. Focusing on their emotional drivers, work-based or otherwise, will often mean driving advocacy of like-minded people.

Integrating Advocacy Incentives into QBRs

Building advocacy incentives into your business strategy requires careful planning and execution. Quarterly Business Reviews (QBRs) present an ideal opportunity to introduce advocacy incentives. These regular check-ins with clients are not just for reviewing past performance and setting future goals, but also for strengthening relationships and exploring collaborative growth opportunities. But how do you do it without sounding desperate, overly salesy, or coming across as if you just want leads and referrals.

Here are a few steps to introduce the incentives in your QBRs and maintaining the relationship.

Setting the Stage for Advocacy
During a QBR, after discussing the usual metrics and KPIs, transition the conversation to the value the customer has experienced. Share success stories and highlight how their journey can inspire others. This is ideal when in the Time to Value, or Time to Show aspects of the QBR. This sets a natural stage for discussing advocacy.

Broaching the Subject
Introduce the concept of advocacy incentives by aligning them with the customer's success. Frame it as an extension of their success story:
"We've seen how much you've achieved with our solution. We believe your insights could benefit others in your industry. Would you be interested in sharing your experiences?"

Engagement and Onboarding
Once a customer shows interest, guide them through the advocacy incentive program. Explain the rewards and recognition they can earn and how their efforts will contribute to the community. Make the process simple and the benefits clear.

Tailoring the Incentive
Customize the advocacy incentives to match the customer's interests and capabilities. For some, public recognition may be a strong motivator, while others might prefer direct rewards like discounts or additional services. Remember the emotional triggers mentioned on the previous pages.

Making Advocacy a Win-Win
Ensure that the advocacy program is mutually beneficial. Customers should feel that their contributions are valued and that they're not just helping you grow, but also gaining something meaningful in return. Latch on to Carmazzi's 8 emotional drivers and identify which one will give them the right feeling.

Follow-Up and Support
After the QBR, provide customers with all the resources they need to be successful advocates. Follow up regularly to support their efforts and to show appreciation for their contributions.

A Strategic QBR Approach

One of our clients during their QBRs often highlights the customer achievements and then introduces their advocacy incentive program. They offer a tiered reward system where customers can earn different levels of incentives based on the number of successful referrals or the quality of testimonials provided. The company supports their advocates with resources like referral links, branded content, and easy-to-share digital assets. As a result, they often see a marked increase in customer engagement and several new leads – I'm sure you know a referral is a hot lead!

Incorporating advocacy incentives into QBRs is a strategic move that can lead to increased brand loyalty and customer engagement. By making advocacy a part of the regular business review process, you normalise it as a key aspect of the customer relationship. This approach not only helps in acquiring new customers through trusted referrals but also deepens existing relationships, creating a community of brand champions who feel valued and empowered.

Advocacy incentives are a powerful strategy for recurring revenue based companies to build brand advocacy, loyalty and drive growth. By rewarding customers who share their love for your product, you not only expand your reach but also deepen the connection with your user base. As we continue to explore the facets of Distinctive Dominance, remember that your customers are your best marketers. Empower them, and they will propel your brand to new heights.

10 Point Checklist for Driving Brand Advocacy

Building brand advocacy is a multifaceted endeavour that requires a strategic approach. Here's a compilation of drivers on how a technology-based business can foster a loyal customer base:

1. **Deliver Consistent Value:** The foundation of brand loyalty is the consistent delivery of value. Ensure that your product not only meets but exceeds customer expectations at every interaction. Regular updates, feature enhancements, and prompt customer support can all contribute to this ongoing value proposition

2. **Personalize Customer Experiences:** Use data analytics to understand customer behaviour and preferences. Personalised experiences make customers feel understood and valued, which can significantly boost loyalty. This could mean tailored recommendations, customized content, or personalized support.

3. **Engage with Customers Beyond Transactions:** Build a relationship with your customers that goes beyond the sale. Engage with them on social media, send them educational content, and involve them in product development through feedback and beta testing opportunities.

4. **Create a Reward System:** Implement a loyalty program that rewards customers for their continued business. This could be through discounts, exclusive access to new features, or rewards for referrals. Make sure the rewards are meaningful and align with your customers' values and needs.

5. **Foster Community:** Encourage customers to become part of a community. This can be facilitated through user groups, forums, or events. A strong community can provide peer support, enhance product knowledge, and create advocates for your brand.

6. **Celebrate Customer Success:** Publicly celebrate milestones and successes achieved by your customers using your product. This not only shows that you value their business but also demonstrates the effectiveness of your solution to other customers.

7. **Provide Exceptional Customer Service:** Customer service can make or break brand loyalty. Ensure that your customer service team is responsive, empathetic, and empowered to solve problems. A positive customer service experience can turn a dissatisfied customer into a loyal advocate.

8. **Solicit and Act on Feedback:** Show customers that their opinions matter by actively seeking out and acting on their feedback. This can help improve the product and the customer experience, and customers will appreciate seeing their suggestions come to life.

9. **Maintain Transparency:** Be honest and open with your customers about changes, challenges, and developments within your company. Transparency builds trust, and trust is a key component of loyalty.

10. **Champion Customer Success:** Make customer success a part of your company culture. When customers achieve their goals with your product, they associate those successes with your brand, reinforcing loyalty and building advocacy.

By integrating these strategies into your business model, you can create a strong foundation for brand advocacy that will support long-term customer relationships and sustained business growth.

Conclusion

As we conclude our exploration of Distinctive Dominance, it's crucial to recognize that this force is not a static achievement but a dynamic process. It's about continuously carving out a unique space in the market, understanding and leveraging your competitive advantage, and nurturing the relationships that turn customers into advocates.

Distinctive Dominance is the culmination of understanding your unique/distinctive value proposition, empowering your team, and delivering on the promise of your brand. It's about creating a narrative of success that resonates with your customers, making them not just users of your product but champions of your vision.

Remember, the journey to achieving Distinctive Dominance is iterative and requires a commitment to excellence, innovation, and customer-centricity. It's a strategic orchestration of insight agility, client centricity, and the other forces we've discussed, all working in concert to elevate your business above the competition.

As you move forward, keep these principles at the forefront of your strategy. Continually refine your approach, listen to your customers, and stay agile. With Distinctive Dominance as your guiding force, you'll be well-equipped to not just survive but thrive, even in the most challenging economic climates.

In the next section of our book, we'll delve into the next transformative force Emotional intelligence, ensuring that you have a comprehensive blueprint for success in the SaaS industry. Stay tuned as we continue to build on these foundations, providing you with the tools and strategies needed to achieve and maintain a position of leadership in your market.

5
Eq

Force 5: Emotional Intelligence

5

Eq

Contents

Emotional Intelligence

At school, you are often taught that the left side of your brain controls the right side of your body and vice versa, but those two hemispheres also control different parts of how your mind works, specifically how you think things through and make decisions. The left side of your brain gives you the capacity to think in words. It performs linear thinking and sequencing and is concerned with logic and facts when making decisions, i.e. the rational. If you excel at maths, thank the left side of your brain which is where mathematics is processed. Meanwhile, the right side of your brain is concentrating on feelings and visualization.

Your imagination is birthed from the right hemisphere, along with things that you know are true but you can't explain - like your intuition, your sense of rhythm, and your ability to create artistically. This breakdown of functionality in your brain was first discovered by Nobel Prize winner Roger W. Sperry, a psychobiologist, back in the 1960s. By being more creative, the right side is also more emotional.

So what? If we take the concept of the left and right brain and apply it to sales, we can consider two parts of the sale –

1. The structured and logical sales proposition and
2. How the customer feels about it.

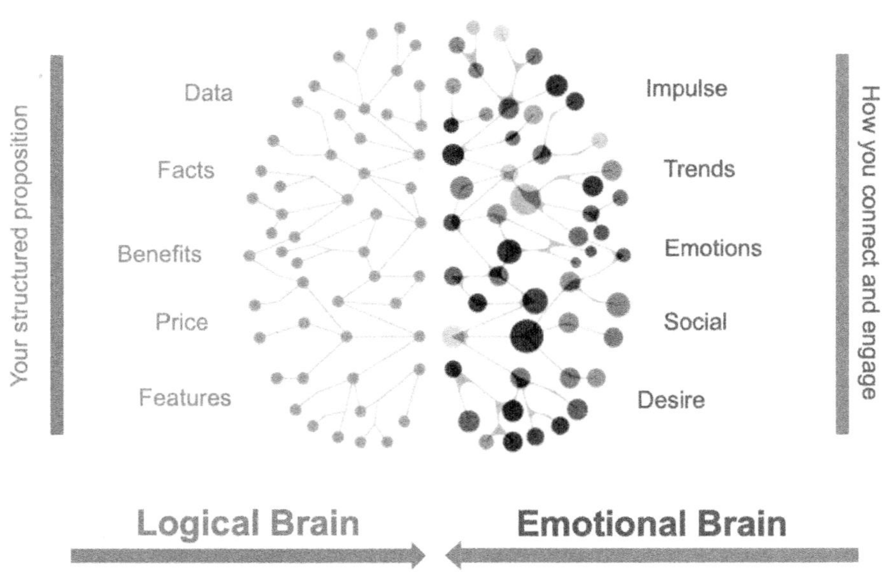

IQ vs EQ

IQ, or Intelligence Quotient, serves as an indicator of a person's mental acuity, ranging from average to exceptional levels, including what is often referred to as genius. Educational systems typically focus on imparting knowledge and evaluating students on their retention and application of this information, assigning grades as an indicator of intellectual prowess. While some students thrive in this academic evaluation, others demonstrate their strengths in different areas of the school experience, like sports, drama, arts, or music.

In the realm of sales, the emphasis is placed on crafting a compelling value proposition. This involves ensuring that the product is logical, fulfils customer needs, provides value, and yields a beneficial return on investment.

Everywhere you look there are some interesting deals to be had, a myriad of products to save or give you more time, save you money, or make you money, make you a better life, increase your health and so on. But something inside us acts as a compass, leading us towards or away from certain deals. I don't mean because the offers won't help, it means am I really interested? Is this something I want to invest my time and effort on even though it is financially or physically beneficial?

This emotional, irrational part of the brain forms part of our subconscious mind. It is not conscious thought but more a 'gut feeling'. Harvard Professor Gerald Zaltman identified that up to 95% of all decisions are made in this unconscious part of the mind. Marketeers have been trying to tap into this for generations, product placement on a shelf, colours used on the packaging, and names of products, all designed to conjure up an emotion or affiliation with the product, but salespeople have been somewhat lacking at identifying this key to unlocking an emotional engagement into the deal.

With the latest research into Neuroscience, combined with the learnings from NLP (Neuro-Linguistic Programming) we can develop better ways to engage the customer in to the sale. Yes, the Value Proposition must stack up, if your products and services don't meet the needs of the customer then you are not even in the race. Having a product that meets the need is the prerequisite, but it only gets you to the meeting - its not going to win the deal.

The successful salesperson needs Emotional Intelligence, also known as the emotional quotient (EQ), which encompasses a person's ability to express, control, evaluate, and identify emotions. EQ is widely known to help people become better leaders and team players since they can understand the emotions of the people around them better. The term was first coined in 1985 by Wayne Payne in his doctoral thesis "A Study of Emotion: Developing Emotional Intelligence" and found its way into the popular vernacular in 1995 in a book by Daniel Goleman entitled "Emotional Intelligence - Why it can matter more than IQ."

EQ: A Force in Tech & SaaS Sales

In the high-stakes arena of technology and software sales and leadership, technical acumen and strategic prowess are table stakes. But EQ is a more subtle, often overlooked force that can be the difference between a leader who merely manages and one who truly inspires and thrives, especially in times of economic downturn. This force is the quintessential element that complements and amplifies the impact of the other four forces we've explored: Disruptive Mindset, Insight Agility, Client Centricity, and Distinctive Dominance.

Emotional Intelligence is the undercurrent that enables sales professionals to navigate the complexities of human emotions and relationships, both within their teams and in their interactions with clients. It's the ability to be acutely aware of one's own emotional state and that of others, and to use this awareness to guide thinking, behaviour, and business decisions. In a downturn, when tensions are high and the margin for error is slim, EQ becomes not just useful, but indispensable.

As we delve into the nuances of Emotional Intelligence, we'll explore how self-awareness helps in recognizing one's own biases and limitations, how self-regulation allows for calm and rational decision-making in the face of challenges, and how motivation can be sustained through intrinsic values rather than extrinsic rewards. We'll also examine how empathy can lead to deeper client relationships and more effective team management, and how social skills can build the networks and alliances necessary for long-term success.

By integrating Emotional Intelligence into the fabric of sales and leadership strategies, professionals can create a resonant leadership style that not only withstands the pressures of a downturn but also paves the way for growth and innovation. It's the force that turns a group of individuals into a cohesive, resilient team, and a product into a solution that clients don't just use, but champion.

As we move forward, remember that Emotional Intelligence is not an innate talent, but a set of skills that can be developed and honed. The following chapters will provide actionable insights and strategies to cultivate these skills, ensuring that you are equipped to lead with empathy, clarity, and strategic foresight.

Self-Awareness

Self-awareness is the cornerstone of Emotional Intelligence. It's the ability to recognize and understand your moods, emotions, and drives, as well as their effect on others. In the context of sales and leadership, self-awareness is what enables professionals to assess their strengths and weaknesses honestly, manage their impulses, and understand how their actions affect the team and customer dynamics.

Pressure to perform in a sales environment is always high and having self-awareness helps leaders and salespeople alike, maintain an emotional equilibrium. It allows them to recognize when stress is affecting their decision-making or when their mood may be impacting team morale. By being aware of these internal states, they can take steps to manage them, ensuring that your leadership style remains consistent and supportive, even under duress. Through this chapter, I will look at EQ from both salespeople and sales leaders as I think both are equally important when driving the business and revenue forward.

Recognise your Impact on Others

Self-awareness also extends to understanding how one's behaviour affects others. A leader who can read the room can adapt their approach to meet the team's needs, whether that means providing encouragement during a challenging project or giving space when tensions are high. In customer interactions, this awareness can help tailor communication and negotiation strategies to the client's emotional state, leading to more productive and positive outcomes.

To enhance self-awareness, sales professionals can engage in regular self-reflection, seek feedback from peers and mentors, and practice mindfulness techniques to stay present and attuned to their emotions. Tools like personality assessments and 360-degree feedback can provide valuable insights into how others perceive their actions, offering a more rounded view of their impact on the workplace.

By fostering self-awareness you lay the groundwork for the other components of Emotional Intelligence. You can become a leader who not only understands themselves but also inspires confidence and trust in those around them, creating an environment where both people and business can thrive.

Self-Regulation

Daniel Goleman describes self-regulation as one of the five key components of emotional intelligence. According to Goleman, self-regulation, which is also referred to as self-control or self-management, is the ability to manage one's emotions and impulses effectively.

It involves:

- Being able to control or redirect disruptive impulses and moods,
- The propensity to suspend judgment and think before acting,
- Maintaining standards of honesty and integrity,
- Taking responsibility for personal performance,
- Being adaptable and open to change,
- Having the ability to say no to impulsive urges,
- Feeling comfortable with novel ideas, approaches, and new information.

Goleman emphasises that self-regulation is crucial for achieving emotional well-being and success in various aspects of life, including personal relationships and professional environments. It is not just about managing temper or withholding negative emotions, but also about the proactive cultivation of positive behaviours and mindsets. In the context of tech sales and leadership, self-regulation is also crucial for maintaining professionalism, making rational decisions, and setting a positive example for the team.

Looking at the list you can see quite quickly how self-management and regulation are vitally important when driving sales in both an abundant market and an economic recession.

Mastering your emotional responses can be crucial in determining the outcome of a client negotiation—leading either to a successful agreement or a missed opportunity. In challenging market conditions where securing business becomes more difficult, your ability to restrain the instinct to finalize a deal at any cost can prevent settling for unfavourable terms and instead guide you to step back when necessary.

It's about staying calm under pressure, being adaptable, and handling change with grace. Leaders who exhibit self-regulation don't lash out in stress or allow a bad day to impact their interactions with the team or clients, they can take the time to reflect and determine the best course of action, although easier said then done when you are under enormous pressure.

Self-regulation also contributes to an environment of trust and fairness. When leaders manage their emotions effectively, they create a sense of safety for their teams. Employees are more likely to believe that their leader will make fair decisions and less likely to be concerned about emotional outbursts or favouritism.

Managing self-regulation in a downturn

Lets be honest, an economic downturn can significantly challenge your self-regulation due to the increased pressure to meet sales targets amidst reduced consumer spending. The stress from an increasingly higher pressure on the sales environment can lead to anxiety, frustration, and impulsive behaviour, which can all undermine self-regulation.

Here's how a downturn can impact self-regulation and what you can do to manage these effects:

Effect	Why	Management Strategy
Stress and Anxiety	The pressure to perform can increase stress levels, potentially leading to burnout.	Implement stress-reduction techniques like regular exercise, mindfulness practices, and ensuring adequate rest.
Frustration and Disappointment	Repeated rejections and failed deals can lead to frustration or a negative mindset.	Set realistic goals, acknowledge efforts regardless of outcomes, and practice positive self-talk.
Impulse to Close Deals	Desperation to make sales can lead to hastily closing deals that may not be in the best interest of the salesperson or the client.	Practice patience and maintain a clear set of ethical standards and deal criteria.
Difficulty in Decision Making	High pressure can cloud judgment, making it difficult to make informed decisions.	Take the time to analyze decisions thoroughly, perhaps discuss options with a mentor or manager.
Decreased Motivation	A continuous negative market can dampen motivation and drive.	Focus on personal development, learn new skills, or improve product knowledge to enhance confidence.
Poor Time Management	In an effort to make more sales, time management may suffer, leading to inefficiency.	Prioritize tasks, create structured schedules, and set aside time for high-value activities.

Strategies for Improving Self-Regulation

Improving self-regulation involves becoming more conscious of one's emotional triggers and developing strategies to deal with them. This could include taking a moment to breathe before responding to a stressful email, practising relaxation techniques, or finding healthy outlets for emotions outside of work.

Managing self-regulation especially during an economic downturn, a salesperson might consider integrating several nuanced practices into their professional routine.

To begin, **embracing a growth mindset** could prove essential. This perspective allows one to view challenges as fertile ground for development, transforming obstacles into opportunities to enhance resilience and fortify skills. Such an outlook encourages a focus on progress and learning, where every setback is a lesson and every success a moment to build upon. We discussed the idea of continuous improvement and the concept of a growth mindset in a few of the previous forces, especially in Force 2, where we discussed that by embracing challenges, persisting in the face of setbacks, and learning from criticism, enables you to position yourself not just to respond to market dynamics but to anticipate and shape them, driving innovation and achieving sustainable success.

In tandem with this mindset, engaging in **reflective practice** can significantly bolster your self-regulation. By taking time to contemplate daily interactions and outcomes, you can gain insight into which strategies are effective and which are not, as well as understand your emotional responses to various situations. This practice of introspection helps in identifying emotional triggers and preparing more constructive responses for future encounters.

Building a supportive network is also invaluable. Collaborating with peers, seeking mentorship, and exchanging coping strategies can provide fresh perspectives and emotional support, which is particularly beneficial when navigating the turbulent waters of an economic slump.

Continuous learning stands as another pillar for maintaining equilibrium. Keeping abreast of market trends and dynamically adjusting sales strategies ensures that you remain competitive and adaptable. This habit not only contributes to better sales outcomes but also to a sense of competency and control, which can mitigate stress. That feeling of being in control also stops the feeling of being a victim to circumstance.

Maintaining a work-life balance is just as crucial. By **deliberately carving out time** for personal life, hobbies, and relaxation, a salesperson can ward off burnout and sustain a healthy perspective. A well-rested and fulfilled individual is more likely to exhibit patience, clear judgment, and sustained motivation—traits that underpin effective self-regulation. Again this is easier said than done, especially as we have a need to close business, but it is a really important aspect to make sure you do not spiral, mentally, into a downward trajectory.

Lastly, a focus on cultivating customer relationships can be a beacon during fiscal turmoil. By **prioritizing genuine connections** over short-term gains, sales professionals can foster a base of loyal clients. These relationships often yield repeat business and referrals, which are invaluable during economic downturns, providing a steadier stream of opportunities and a sense of stability and accomplishment that bolsters emotional resilience.

Incorporating these approaches into your professional life doesn't just enhance self-regulation but can also lead to a more satisfying and successful career. Leaders can also set clear values and standards for themselves and their teams, which can serve as a guide for behaviour. When values are clear, decisions become easier, and emotional responses can be more easily managed because there's a framework in place for what's acceptable and what's not.

By mastering self-regulation, you not only improve your own performance but also foster a more productive, harmonious workplace.

As we navigate the complexities of emotional self-regulation, we recognize its profound impact on the workplace atmosphere and decision-making processes. But beyond managing emotions lies the driving force that propels sales professionals toward excellence, I mean motivation. This intrinsic drive is the fuel for persistence, innovation, and the relentless pursuit of goals despite setbacks and challenges. Now, let's delve into the essence of motivation and its pivotal role in shaping the path to success.

Motivation

Motivation in the sales world is not just about hitting sales targets or closing deals, it's the inner drive that pushes individuals to go beyond the mundane and strive for the extraordinary. It's what compels a salesperson to understand the deeper needs of their clients, or a leader to inspire their team to reach new heights.

Intrinsic & Extrinsic Motivation

Intrinsic and extrinsic motivation are two fundamental types of motivation that can drive behaviour and performance.

Intrinsic motivation comes from within the individual. It is driven by personal satisfaction, interest, or enjoyment in the task itself. For salespeople, intrinsic motivation might be derived from the pleasure of connecting with new people, the satisfaction of helping customers solve problems, or the intellectual challenge of navigating complex sales processes. When a salesperson is intrinsically motivated, they work on tasks because they find them rewarding in and of themselves, not because of an external reward.

Extrinsic motivation, on the other hand, refers to motivation that is derived from outside the individual. Common extrinsic motivators include monetary rewards, bonuses, commissions, recognition, status, and promotions. In the sales context, extrinsic motivation is often tied to targets and results. For example, salespeople may push themselves to secure a deal for the sake of a bonus or to avoid negative outcomes such as job loss or reduced income.

The importance of understanding intrinsic and extrinsic motivation in the realm of sales cannot be overstated. Sales roles often come with a high degree of uncertainty and rejection, which can be demoralising. Those who are intrinsically motivated are typically more resilient in the face of these challenges because their motivation comes from a deeper, more personal place. They're able to push through tough times because their drive is not solely dependent on the next sale or commission cheque.

During an economic downturn, the distinction between these types of motivation becomes even more critical. Extrinsic motivators, particularly financial incentives, may diminish as sales targets become harder to hit and companies cut back on bonuses and raises. If a salesperson relies solely on extrinsic rewards, they may struggle to maintain motivation during such periods. However, those with strong intrinsic motivation are more likely to continue to perform effectively, even in tougher economic times. They can sustain their motivation through the internal satisfaction they get from their work, which is not directly impacted by the external economic environment.

Moreover, in difficult economic conditions, customers may tighten their budgets and become more discerning with their purchases, making the sales process more challenging. Salespeople who are intrinsically motivated can be more focused on meeting the true needs of their customers rather than just closing a sale, which can lead to stronger relationships and increased trust. This approach will obviously pay off in the long term, as customers are more likely to return to salespeople they perceive as helpful and authentic, particularly when economic conditions improve.

Thus, while extrinsic rewards can provide short-term motivation and are important in their own right, fostering intrinsic motivation among sales staff is crucial for long-term success and resilience, especially in the face of economic adversity.

Cultivating a Motivated Mindset

Cultivating a motivated mindset means finding passion in your work, setting challenging yet achievable goals, and celebrating the small victories along the way. It's about fostering a culture where curiosity is encouraged, and learning is continuous.

Cultivating a growth mindset and maintaining motivation, whether through intrinsic or extrinsic factors, during an economic downturn can be a challenging yet vital endeavour for all.

Self-Driven Strategies (Intrinsic)

In the face of economic challenges, a salesperson's intrinsic motivation becomes their anchor. It's the inner drive that compels them to pursue their goals, regardless of external rewards or pressures. This self-sustained motivation is fuelled by personal growth, mastery of the task, and the inherent satisfaction derived from the work itself. By focusing on personal development, setting achievable goals, and finding fulfilment in the journey rather than just the destination, sales professionals can maintain a strong internal focus of control. This segment of the model underscores the importance of resilience, adaptability, and a commitment to relationship-building as core components that empower salespeople to thrive from within.

Here are several approaches a salesperson can take to foster a growth and motivated mindset in tough economic times:

Embracing Learning:	Salespeople can take personal initiative to engage in continuous learning. This personal growth is inherently rewarding and enhances self-efficacy.
Setting Personal Goals:	Individuals can create their own set of achievable micro-goals, which serve to provide internal satisfaction upon completion.
Process Orientation:	Sales professionals can focus on the quality of their sales process rather than fixating on the outcomes. This encourages a sense of control and satisfaction from personal improvement.
Resilience & Adaptability:	Individuals can work on personal resilience, viewing challenges as opportunities for growth, and adaptability to change, which are crucial for intrinsic motivation.
Relationship Building:	Salespeople can invest in building and nurturing authentic relationships with clients, finding satisfaction in the deeper connections made, irrespective of immediate sales outcomes.
Self-Reflection:	Improving self-awareness and emotional regulation is a personal endeavour that contributes to a salesperson's intrinsic motivation by helping them manage stress and connect with clients.

Managerial and Organisational Support (Extrinsic)

While intrinsic motivation is critical, the role of extrinsic factors, i.e. those external incentives and structures provided by managers and organisations, cannot be understated. These are the elements that can ignite a sales team's drive and sustain their performance through recognition, support, and rewards. This part of the model highlights how a supportive environment can stimulate a salesperson's motivation through timely feedback, recognition of effort, and the fostering of professional growth. Mentorship programs, rewards for dedication, and an emphasis on work-life balance are all extrinsic factors that, when aligned with a salesperson's intrinsic desires, create a synergistic effect that can propel a team to success, even when external economic conditions are less than favourable.

Consider the following:

Feedback and Recognition:	Managers should provide constructive feedback and recognize the efforts of their sales team, which acts as an external motivator, driving performance.
Mentorship Programs:	Organizations can establish mentorship programs to provide guidance and support, aiding professional growth which can have motivational effects.
Rewarding Effort:	Even when sales targets are not met, managers can find ways to reward the hard work and dedication of their salespeople to maintain motivation.
Work-Life Balance:	Companies can create policies that support a healthy work-life balance, preventing burnout and keeping morale high.
Information Sharing:	Managers can ensure sales teams are well-informed about market conditions and encourage strategic flexibility, helping them feel supported and prepared to face market challenges.

In this model, the intrinsic strategies revolve around personal development and satisfaction from internal achievements, while the extrinsic strategies rely on the environment created by managers and the organization to encourage and reward the desired behaviours and outcomes. Together, they form a comprehensive approach to maintaining motivation during economic downturns.

Strategies for Sustaining Motivation

Sustaining motivation, especially during tough economic times, requires resilience and adaptability. Encouraging a growth mindset, where challenges are seen as opportunities to learn, can help maintain high levels of motivation. Additionally, ensuring that team members understand the impact of their work and how it contributes to the larger picture can keep motivation strong.

The Importance of Resilience

Resilience and adaptability in the sales profession are often bantered around like buzzwords but they're the cornerstones of sustained success and well-being. The pressure to meet quotas and manage challenging client interactions is a daily reality in sales and underscores the need for resilience, which is a quality that enables salespeople to bounce back and maintain their drive in the face of setbacks. This resilience ensures a steady hand on the tiller, keeping performance levels consistent over time.

However, in an industry as dynamic as sales, where the only constant is change, adaptability is equally vital. It's the adaptability that allows salespeople to adjust their sails when market winds shift, adopting new strategies and technologies to keep moving forward. This flexibility not only keeps salespeople relevant but sparks innovation, helping them to stand out in a crowded market.

Building a culture of resilience

In fostering resilience, organisations play a crucial role. A positive work environment acts as a breeding ground for tenacity, where each small victory is celebrated, and every effort is acknowledged, creating a buffer against the strain of the job. When salespeople feel supported and appreciated, they are more likely to take risks and show initiative, contributing to a culture of resilience.

Moreover, resilience thrives on autonomy. People who feel they have a hand in steering their own careers are more inclined to embrace the lessons of both triumph and failure. Providing resources for professional growth further equips them to face the ever-changing tides with confidence.

Developing emotional intelligence is akin to equipping salespeople with navigational tools that are crucial when traversing emotional landscapes, both their own and those of their clients. Training in emotional intelligence can guide them in managing emotions effectively, a skill that is at the heart of resilience. Encouraging sales professionals to engage in reflection allows them to understand their experiences deeply. This reflective practice can be as simple as keeping a journal or as structured as coaching sessions. Either way, it instils a habit of learning from the past to improve future outcomes.

Mental and Physical Health

No journey can be sustained without due care for the traveller's well-being. Promoting a balance between work and personal life, and providing support for physical and mental health, can safeguard against the hazards of burnout. It's about creating a holistic approach to the well-being of salespeople, ensuring they have the stamina to continue their journey, no matter the weather.

In the book "The Power of Full Engagement: Managing Energy, Not Time" by Jim Loehr and Tony Schwartz, they state that prioritising self-care such as taking steps to maintain their physical and emotional health, such as exercise, healthy eating, and adequate sleep, is the key to high performance and personal renewal.

This sounds easy but isn't, and also sounds quite soft, but isn't. When times are tougher, managers tend to want people to work harder, which, unfortunately, is sometimes measured by the clock! Get people coming in early, going home late and burning the midnight oil. Let's not pretend it won't happen, and sometimes it needs to happen, but there must be a counterbalance to offset those long hard days. You must build into the flow some time to allow for a mental and physical release. Don't scrimp on the offsites, and team days, and don't fill them full of briefings. Find time to make them fun and make time for play. The team needs it.

In a narrative of resilience and adaptability, the successful salesperson is both the protagonist who endures and the innovator who transforms. The pulsing heart of motivation not only drives us towards our goals but also connects us to the human element of our work. It's here, at the intersection of ambition and compassion, that empathy emerges as a cornerstone of emotional intelligence.

Empathy, the ability to understand and share the feelings of another, is not a soft skill, it's a strategic asset that can forge deeper connections, foster trust, and lead to more meaningful customer interactions. In the next chapter, we will explore how empathy can be harnessed to enhance relationships and drive success in the competitive world of sales.

Empathy

In an economic downturn, we need to evolve the usual 'Value Based Selling' approaches to become more in tune with the customer and demonstrate empathy for the situation. However, there is a thin line between being a 'hard sell' and being so empathetic that we simply don't sell or even try.

3 Types of Empathy

Empathy, at its core, is the ability to understand and share the feelings of another person. It's a fundamental component of human interaction that allows us to connect with others on a deeper emotional level. In the context of sales, empathy enables sales professionals to build rapport with clients, understand their unique challenges and needs, and offer solutions that resonate on a personal level.

Daniel Goleman first introduced three types of empathy in his book "Social Intelligence: The New Science of Human Relationships," published in 2006. This book expands on the ideas of emotional intelligence that he discussed in his earlier works and explores the social aspects of emotional intelligence, including empathy.

He introduced 3 types of empathy:

Cognitive Empathy: This is the ability to understand how a person feels and what they might be thinking. Cognitive empathy helps in negotiations and in motivating people because it gives an insight into the other person's mindset and emotions. It's about perspective-taking and understanding the other person's point of view.

Emotional Empathy: This type of empathy refers to the ability to physically feel another person's emotions, almost as if the emotions were contagious. This is what helps people build emotional connections with others. Emotional empathy makes someone more personable and relatable.

Compassionate Empathy: Also known as empathic concern, this goes beyond simply understanding others and sharing their feeling, it moves a person to act, to help however they can. In a business context, this might involve going the extra mile to help a customer solve a problem or meet a need.

In the context of sales, accentuated during an economic downturn, all three types of empathy play a crucial role. Cognitive empathy allows you to understand the business challenges your clients face. Emotional empathy helps you build a personal connection and show genuine concern for the client's situation. Compassionate empathy can drive you to work diligently on behalf of the client, finding solutions that truly serve the client's needs and alleviate their challenges.

The Organisational Amygdala Response

Okay, a quick piece of science - the amygdala is an almond-shaped set of neurons located deep in the brain's medial temporal lobe. It is a crucial part of the limbic system, which is involved in many of our emotions and motivations, particularly those that are related to survival. The amygdala is best known for its role in processing fear, though it plays a part in other emotional responses as well.

When faced with uncertainty or a potential threat, the amygdala can trigger a fight, flight, or freeze response:

FIGHT	FLIGHT	FREEZE
This response occurs when the amygdala signals that a threat must be confronted. Hormones like adrenaline and cortisol are released, preparing the body for action. This can manifest as aggression or assertiveness in a business context, as individuals or organisations push back against the perceived threat. "We will trade out of this!"	The flight response is the desire to escape the threat. In a business setting, this might look like withdrawing from a market, cutting back on investment, or abandoning a project. "Batten down the hatches!"	Sometimes, neither fight nor flight seems like a viable option, and the amygdala triggers a freeze response. This can be a temporary state of inaction while the person or organisation assesses the situation. In the business world, this might involve delaying decisions, putting projects on hold, or a general slowdown in activity as the company tries to understand the changing environment. "let's wait and see!"

These responses are deeply ingrained survival mechanisms. In modern settings, they can be triggered not just by physical threats but by psychological and social threats as well, such as financial loss, reputational damage, or strategic threats to a business.

In times of economic downturn or uncertainty, organisations and individuals may experience heightened activity in the amygdala, leading to more pronounced fight, flight, or freeze responses. This can impact decision-making, risk assessment, and strategic planning. Being aware of these responses and understanding how to manage them is crucial for maintaining rational, strategic decision-making during such periods.

Empathetic Approach

No matter which mode they take on, to continue to do business and make sales, the organisation, including the sales and marketing teams, need to demonstrate empathy with the customers. Doing so will uncover more about the challenges and environment, and build deeper rapport, if you are ever going to engage the customer into entertaining the notion of spending money and driving change. This means that your messaging and approach must be empathetic and demonstrate that you understand, you feel it, and you are moved to help!

Utilising the other forces mapped out already, Disruptive Mindset, Insight Agility, Client Centricity and Distinctive Dominance, demonstrating empathy in each of these aspects will be crucial in establishing rapport and building trust.

Cognitive Empathy

In the realm of cognitive empathy, it's all about delving into the customer's mindset. Salespeople should immerse themselves in active listening during interactions, ensuring they absorb not just the words but the underlying sentiments and priorities. This approach is complemented by asking insightful questions that probe deeper into the customer's challenges and goals. It's not just about understanding their situation but also showing respect and validation for their perspectives, which fosters trust and a stronger connection.

Consider the following:

- Conducting in-depth market research to understand the customer's industry, competitors, and market trends.
- Preparing tailored questions that probe into the customer's specific challenges and goals.
- Actively listening during conversations, not just to respond but to truly understand the customer's viewpoint.
- Demonstrating an understanding of the customer's business language and key performance indicators.

In essence you need to show the customer you get it – and understand.

Emotional Empathy

Emotional empathy takes the sales relationship to a more personal level. It involves a keen sensitivity to the customer's emotional state. When a customer expresses frustration or excitement, acknowledging and reflecting these emotions shows that you're not just a salesperson but someone who genuinely understands and cares. Personalising interactions to align with their emotional state and maintaining authenticity in your concern can create a lasting impact.

Emotional empathy is the ability to feel what the customer is feeling. It's about creating a genuine emotional connection. Develop this connection by:

- Paying close attention to the customer's tone, language, and non-verbal cues to gauge their emotional state.
- Reflecting the customer's emotions in their responses, such as sharing their excitement or acknowledging their frustrations.
- Sharing relevant personal experiences or stories that resonate with the customer's situation, builds a deeper bond.
- Maintaining a genuine and authentic demeanour, ensuring that the customer feels heard and understood on a personal level.

Use matching and mirroring techniques to continue to build rapport and build the relationship. Spot emotional triggers and cues, that show you how the customer is feeling (as discussed in Distinctive Dominance), and use Emotional Adjectives in your problem-based questions to help the customer express their emotions (as discussed in Client Centricity).

Compassionate Empathy

Finally, compassionate empathy is about translating understanding into tangible support. It's where salespeople offer solutions that are not just products but real answers to the customer's problems. This empathy is extended beyond the sale through consistent support, regular check-ins, and providing resources that empower the customer. It's a commitment to not just understand or feel with the customer but to be an active participant in their success journey.

Compassionate empathy goes beyond understanding and feeling, it's about actively contributing to the customer's success. This involves:

- Offering solutions that are closely aligned with the customer's needs and challenges, demonstrating a commitment to their success.
- Following up after sales to ensure the customer is satisfied and to offer additional support or resources.
- Being proactive in addressing potential issues or challenges the customer might face with the product or service.
- Creating a supportive environment where the customer feels they can reach out with concerns or questions at any time.

When moving into the solution mode, do not fast-track past the pains and issues uncovered. Play back the problems and demonstrate active listening but also then show how your product or service will help mitigate both the problems and help build for a better future. Utilise the Hypnotic Heartbeat discussed in the Disruptive Mindset section on reframing.

Remember Empathy is not sympathy. With the right balance of the 3 empathies listed, you will be able to engage with customers and genuinely help them overcome some of their challenges. To make the most of these different types of empathy, organisations and individuals need to harness all three in their interaction with customers, and colleagues. It will enable you to get deeper into their problems and needs, help them understand Why to Change, and lead them to the Why to do it Now.

Listening as a SuperPower

When we take the time to truly listen to someone, it creates a sense of emotional connection that's hard to replicate. Imagine how it feels when someone gives you their undivided attention, it's as if they're right there with you, fully engaged in every word you say, genuinely interested in your thoughts, and making an effort to understand your perspective. This act of being present, of listening attentively, weaves a stronger bond between two people, making each interaction more meaningful.

It's a bit ironic, though, isn't it? Just as listening can draw us closer, the lack of it can push us miles apart. When our words seem to fall on deaf ears, it can leave us feeling disregarded and even provoke annoyance or anger, especially if it's clear that the other person has missed the point, or their body language screams disinterest. It's the lack of empathy or concern that drives us insane.

In today's whirlwind of distractions, where every gadget and gizmo vie for our attention, choosing to shut out the world and focus on the person in front of us is a challenge. It's an art really, to give someone your complete attention and remain intrigued by what they have to say.

Now, throw in the dynamics of being a salesperson. You're there to engage with a customer, to make your pitch, to close a deal. So even as they speak, part of your mind might be racing ahead, plotting the next question or crafting the perfect response to show how you can fulfil their needs. Balancing the act of listening with the need to sell is a delicate dance—one that requires patience, practice, and a genuine interest in the stories each customer brings to the table.

5 Types of Listening

Before getting into listening for your customer's emotional drivers let's take a moment to look at 5 different types of listening.

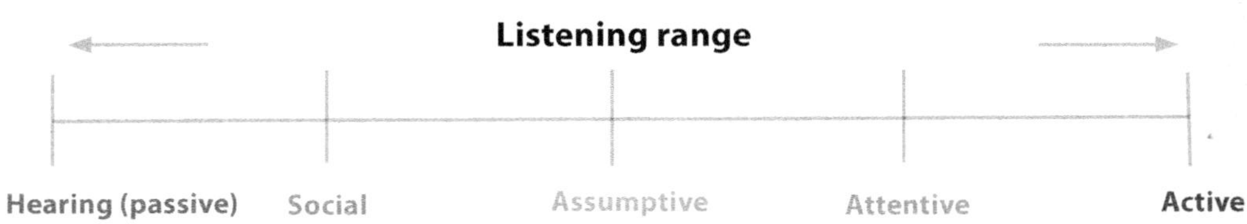

Let's journey through the world of listening. Think back to those early days of hearing tests, with the clunky headphones and the school nurse's expectant gaze. You'd wait for those beeps and boops, raising a hand obediently when a sound whispered into one ear. This, my friend, is what we'd call **passive listening**—the basic acknowledgement that yes, the mechanics of hearing are in working order. It's listening at its most fundamental, devoid of any deeper engagement.

Now, transport yourself to a buzzing social scene—perhaps a lively party or a bustling family gathering. The air is a mosaic of chit-chat, laughter, and the clinking of glasses. Here, your ears flit from one thread of dialogue to another, occasionally latching onto a snippet that piques your interest. Or perhaps it's the radio chattering away as you potter around the house, providing a comforting backdrop until a catchy tune or a riveting news headline hooks your attention. This ebb and flow of attention we call **social listening**.

But here comes a traditional one, associated with many salespeople, **assumptive listening**. You've likely encountered this on the receiving end or, dare I say, as the perpetrator. It's when a question is posed, not to seek an answer, but as a springboard for one's own assumptions. "I bet I know what you're going to say..." is the hallmark of this listening style. Sales folks, beware! Falling into this trap means you might be tuning out potential clients, all the while fishing for that glossy brochure, ready to pounce with your pitch instead of truly engaging.

Ascending the listening ladder, we arrive at **attentive listening**. This is where the magic happens. In this space, you're fully present with the other person, soaking in their words, making notes, maintaining that all-important eye contact. You nod, you murmur those little affirmations—"Ah, I see," "Yes," "Go on"—that tell the speaker they have your full attention. It's not just about hearing them out, it's about engaging, asking questions that show you're not just a passive recipient of information but an active participant in the conversation.

Active Listening

For a lot of people, the 'Attentive' listening above was what they had been taught as 'Active Listening', i.e. listen and respond. Active listening takes a lot more work as rather than listening to what the customer is saying, the focus of being Active is to ensure you are listening to the story and trying to ascertain why the story is the story.

Consider what your mind is doing when it is listening to someone sharing their story or point of view? Interestingly as it is listening it can be checking your own references to see if you have a similar viewpoint, experiences, and thoughts.

The challenge when we are trying to Active Listening is to switch this off, otherwise you will potentially miss what they are truly saying and therefore run the risk of using assumptive listening.

In his 2003 book, Marshall Rosenberg describes four basic "filters" or ways of interpreting communication that can interfere with clear understanding and connection: (1) judgments and evaluations, (2) comparisons, (3) demands, and (4) attributions of motive. He suggests that becoming aware of these filters and learning to communicate in a more empathic and compassionate way can help to create more meaningful and fulfilling relationships.

Judgments and Evaluations: When we listen to others through a lens of judgment, we often evaluate their words against our own set of beliefs and standards. This filter leads us to label and categorize what's being said as 'good' or 'bad,' 'right' or 'wrong,' which can create a defensive response and close down open dialogue. The challenge is to recognise our own internal responses and to separate them from what's actually being communicated, allowing for a non-judgmental space where understanding can flourish.

Comparisons: Engaging in comparisons while listening can be an obstacle to empathy and understanding. This happens when we measure individuals against others or against idealised standards. It can lead to feelings of inadequacy or superiority, jealousy or resentment. Instead of comparing, Rosenberg advocates for appreciating everyone's unique qualities and contributions, which helps in fostering a more accepting and connected interaction.

Demands: When expressions come across as demands rather than requests, it can create a dynamic of win/lose, with one party feeling pressured or coerced. This perception turns what could be a collaborative exchange into a contest of wills. Rosenberg suggests reframing demands into requests that acknowledge the other person's needs and willingness, paves the way for cooperation and mutual respect.

Attributions of Motive: This filter involves making assumptions about why someone is saying or doing something—assigning motives without clarity. Such attributions can be coloured by our past experiences, fears, or biases and often do not reflect the true intentions of the speaker. To avoid misunderstandings that this filter can cause, Rosenberg recommends engaging in dialogue that seeks to understand the actual motivations behind words and actions, asking questions and expressing our own feelings and needs openly.

Don't judge me!

As the person starts to share with you the story, your brain listens, and you get this inner voice that starts talking to you; "I wouldn't have done that, that's not how to do it, that interesting, I know the answer to this, I've heard this before, this is to do with..." In essence, you listen to the story and you are looking for answers. The brain is in judgement mode, it is judging what they are telling you and trying to figure out the problem or find the solution. This is a good thing, but whilst it is doing that, it is moving into a more social listening capacity, or the synapses of the brain keep flicking between listening and processing.

To truly listen, you need to turn off this inner voice and listen to the words, the tonality, and the body language, but how do you do that and how do you know when to engage and speak?

3 Levels of Active Listening

John Medina stated our brain runs on 12 watts of power and uses about 20% of the body's energy when it is in a rest state. Therefore, it is designed to run as efficiently as possible, almost in tick-over, and will not fire up the brain unless it is necessary. Therefore, to truly get to understand your customer, and actively listen, you need to engage the customer, get the brain to fire up, and then look and listen for the emotional aspects, as well as the thoughts of the customer. That is the left and the right brain activity.

As a psychological framework that helps understand how we process and respond to information consider that the brain has 3 levels of accessing information:

Level 1 – Fast Logic

This level represents our brain's immediate, instinctive reactions to stimuli. It's often referred to as the "fast thinking" process in Daniel Kahneman's dual-process theory (think fast and slow). At this level, the brain makes quick judgments and decisions based on heuristics or mental shortcuts. These responses are typically automatic, driven by emotions or ingrained biases, and don't require much conscious thought. This level is useful for routine decisions or when quick action is needed, but it can also lead to errors or biases in judgment.

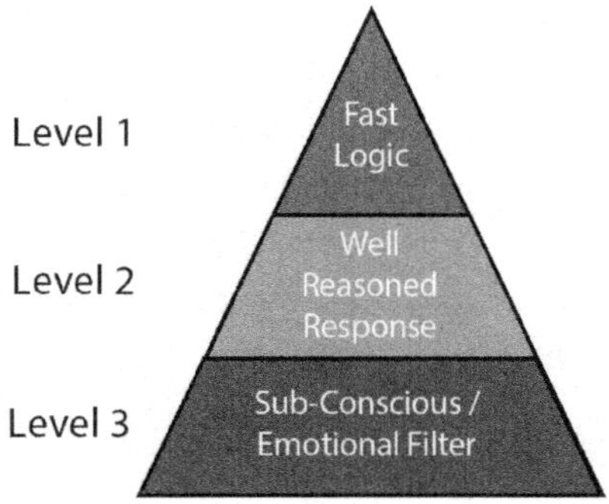

Level 2 - Well-Reasoned Response:

This level involves more deliberate and conscious thinking. It's where we engage in rational analysis, weigh options, and consider the consequences of our actions. This "slow thinking" process, also described by Kahneman, requires more cognitive effort and is used for more complex decision-making tasks. At this level, we're more likely to consider evidence, logic, and reason, making it a more reliable but slower process.

Level 3 - Subconscious Level:

This level refers to the processes and activities of the brain that occur below the level of conscious awareness. The subconscious mind influences our beliefs, habits, and underlying attitudes. It's a reservoir of feelings, thoughts, urges, and memories that are outside of our conscious awareness. The subconscious mind can play a significant role in influencing our behaviour and reactions, often in ways we're not fully aware of. Accessing and understanding this level can lead to deeper insights into our motivations and behaviours.

In the context of sales and customer interactions, being aware of these levels can be crucial. For instance, a salesperson might use Level 1 thinking to quickly adapt to a customer's mood or immediate needs, Level 2 thinking to logically present a product's benefits, and an understanding of Level 3 to connect with deeper customer motivations or address subconscious concerns.

Understanding these levels of brain processing is important for active listening, especially in contexts like sales, negotiations, or customer relations. Here's how each level relates to active listening:

> **Level 1 - Fast Logic or Noise:** This level involves instinctive reactions and immediate judgments. In active listening, it's important to be aware of these instinctive responses and consciously set them aside. Quick judgments or assumptions can hinder truly understanding the speaker's perspective. Active listening requires suspending these immediate reactions to fully engage with and understand the speaker's message.
>
> **Level 2 - Well-Reasoned Response:** This level of processing is critical in active listening. It involves consciously processing what the speaker is saying, analysing their words, and understanding the context and content of their message. This level of listening

allows for a thoughtful, well-considered response, rather than a reactive one. It's where you interpret the speaker's words, consider their implications, and formulate an appropriate reply.

Level 3 - Subconscious Level: Understanding and being aware of the subconscious level can enhance active listening by allowing you to pick up on non-verbal cues, underlying emotions, and unspoken concerns. The subconscious mind can influence both the speaker's communication and the listener's interpretation. Being attuned to this level can lead to a deeper understanding of the speaker's true feelings and intentions, which might not be explicitly stated.

In summary, effective active listening involves managing your immediate, instinctive reactions (Level 1), engaging in thoughtful analysis and understanding (Level 2), and being sensitive to the underlying, subconscious elements of communication (Level 3). This comprehensive approach ensures a more empathetic, accurate, and effective communication process.

Having explored the depths of empathy and the significance of active listening and self-regulation, we now turn our attention to another vital component of Emotional Intelligence: social skills. In the challenging landscape of an economic downturn, the ability to navigate social interactions effectively becomes even more crucial. Social skills in a business context are not just about being friendly or personable; they encompass a range of competencies that enable sales professionals to build strong relationships, influence decisions, and foster a collaborative environment. These skills are the glue that binds all other aspects of Emotional Intelligence, allowing for the creation of meaningful connections and the cultivation of trust with clients and colleagues alike.

The key to utlising social skills and true active listening will enable you to utilise your emotional intelligence to read the customer, pick up on the emotional triggers and begin to steer the customer through better use of empathy.

Conclusion

As we conclude our exploration of Emotional Intelligence, it's crucial to recognize the transformative impact it has on both the sales process and the overall success of a business. Emotional Intelligence is not just an abstract concept, and it is certainly not light and fluffy. It's a practical, powerful tool that, when harnessed effectively, can significantly elevate the way sales professionals connect with, understand, and serve their clients, especially in challenging economic times.

We delved into the core components of Emotional Intelligence: self-awareness, self-regulation, motivation, empathy, and social skills. Each of these elements plays a vital role in shaping a salesperson's ability to navigate complex emotional landscapes, build stronger relationships, and ultimately, achieve sales success. By mastering these skills, sales professionals can create a more resonant and effective sales approach, one that is attuned to the nuanced needs and emotions of their clients.

In an economic downturn, where uncertainty and stress are prevalent, the ability to empathize with clients, regulate one's own emotional responses, and maintain a positive, motivated outlook becomes critical. It's these skills that enable sales teams to not just survive but thrive, turning potential challenges into opportunities for growth and deeper client engagement.

Moreover, Emotional Intelligence fosters a culture of understanding and adaptability within organizations. It encourages a more collaborative, supportive environment, essential for innovation and resilience in the face of market shifts and economic pressures.

The lessons and insights gained from this exploration of Emotional Intelligence are not just confined to this section; they permeate every aspect of a successful, forward-thinking sales strategy. In the chapters that follow, we'll see how these emotional skills intertwine with other forces, creating a comprehensive, robust approach to dominating in a downturn.

forces
5

COMBINED FORCES

THE
QUINTESSENTIAL FUSION

Contents

Bringing the Five Forces to Life

The ability to not just adapt but to thrive hinges on a deep understanding and application of five critical forces: Disruptive Mindset, Insight Agility, Client Centricity, Distinctive Dominance, and Emotional Intelligence. Each of these forces, while powerful on their own, can create an unparalleled synergy when integrated effectively. This section delves into the essence of combining these forces within your business, transforming them from abstract concepts into the driving factors of your success.

Imagine each force as an essential ingredient in a complex recipe. Just as in cooking, where the combination of ingredients can create a dish far greater than the sum of its parts, in business, the amalgamation of these forces can lead to outcomes that are exponentially more impactful. For instance, a Disruptive Mindset, when coupled with Insight Agility, empowers businesses to not only foresee changes but also to adapt swiftly and intelligently. Similarly, Client Centricity, when infused with Emotional Intelligence, allows for a deeper, more empathetic understanding of customer needs, leading to stronger, more enduring relationships.

Combined Forces

The true magic lies in the interplay of these forces. A business that cultivates a Disruptive Mindset is naturally inclined to foster Insight Agility, as both require a keen sense of market dynamics and an appetite for innovation. Client Centricity, when practised in an environment that values Emotional Intelligence, leads to a deeper understanding of customer needs and a more authentic connection with them. Distinctive Dominance is not just about being the best in your field, it's about leveraging your unique strengths in a way that resonates with your clients on a deeper level, something that is greatly enhanced by Emotional Intelligence.

In the following sections, we will explore each of these interactions in detail, providing you with a guide on how to weave these forces into the very fabric of your business strategy. This is not just about adopting a new set of tactics, it's about embracing a philosophy that will redefine how you operate, compete, and succeed in the SaaS landscape.

A Dynamic Duo

One thing I have learnt in my business career is that mastering a single strategy or approach is often not enough to ensure success. The real power lies in the synergy created by combining multiple forces, each bringing its unique strengths and perspectives. When we talk about combining two of the Five Forces we're referring to a strategic fusion that amplifies the effectiveness of each individual force.

This concept of combining forces is akin to creating a well-rounded, multi-faceted approach to business challenges and opportunities. It's about leveraging the strengths of one area to complement and enhance the capabilities of another. For instance, merging the forward-thinking approach of a Disruptive Mindset with the data-driven precision of Insight Agility creates a powerhouse for innovation that's both visionary and grounded in reality. Similarly, blending Client Centricity with Emotional Intelligence can lead to deeper, more empathetic customer relationships, enhancing customer loyalty and satisfaction.

The beauty of this approach lies in its flexibility and adaptability. Depending on the specific challenges and goals of a business, different combinations of these forces can be employed to create a tailored strategy. This not only ensures a more holistic approach to problem-solving but also fosters a culture of continuous learning and adaptation.

In the following sections, we'll explore the unique advantages and transformative potential of combining different pairs of these Five Forces, illustrating how they can work together to create a greater impact than any single force could achieve on its own. This integrated approach is key to thriving in today's fast-paced, ever-evolving business landscape.

Let's start by looking at the power of having two of the forces working together. As we work our way up to utilising more forces together you will see the power of having all five in play. I will utilise the power of 2 to show you all the combinations, but as we move onto integrating 3 and 4 together I will give you a couple of examples. Remember the real power is bring them all into play!

Disruptive Mindset & Insight Agility

A disruptive mindset, while powerful on its own, achieves its full potential when coupled with insight agility. Here's an exploration of how these two forces interact and why they are more effective together:

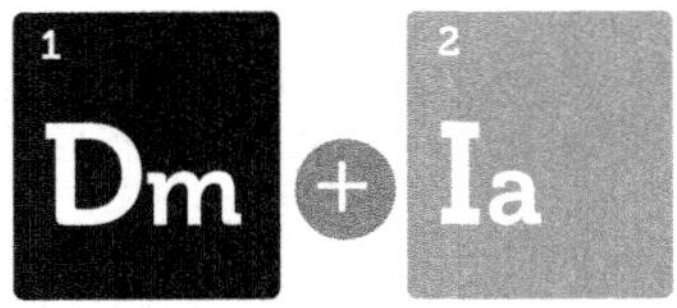

Disruptive Mindset:
The Foundation

Challenging Norms: A disruptive mindset involves questioning and challenging the status quo. It's about looking at problems and opportunities from new angles.

Innovation-Driven: This mindset fosters innovation by encouraging unconventional thinking and a willingness to explore uncharted territories.

Insight Agility:
The Catalyst

Informed Decisions: Insight agility involves the ability to quickly gather, analyse, and act on data and insights. This capability ensures that the innovations and challenges posed by a disruptive mindset are grounded in reality and informed by current market conditions and customer needs.

Adaptability: With insight agility, an organisation can rapidly adapt to changing circumstances, using real-time data to pivot strategies as needed. This adaptability is crucial for the successful implementation of disruptive ideas.

The Synergy

Feasibility and Relevance: A disruptive mindset generates innovative ideas, but insight agility helps in assessing their feasibility and relevance. It ensures that disruptive ideas are not just novel but also viable and aligned with market needs.

Risk Mitigation: While a disruptive mindset can sometimes lead to high-risk propositions, insight agility helps in mitigating these risks by providing a clear understanding of the market and customer dynamics.

Continuous Improvement: Insight agility allows for the continuous testing and refining of disruptive ideas. It enables an organisation to learn quickly from successes and failures, leading to more effective and refined innovations over time.

Conclusion

In isolation, a disruptive mindset might lead to ideas that are either too detached from market realities or unsustainable in the long term. Insight agility, on the other hand, without the drive and creativity of a disruptive mindset, might lead to incremental improvements but miss out on game-changing innovations. Together, they create a powerful combination where creativity is informed and enhanced by real-world insights, leading to innovations that are both groundbreaking and strategically sound.

Client Centricity and Distinctive Dominance

Let's explore how Client Centricity and Distinctive Dominance complement each other and why they are more effective when integrated:

3 Cc + 4 Dd

Client Centricity: The Core

Understanding Needs: Client Centricity revolves around deeply understanding and prioritizing the needs and experiences of customers.

Tailored Solutions: This approach involves creating solutions and experiences that are specifically tailored to meet the unique needs of each client, enhancing satisfaction and loyalty.

Distinctive Dominance: The Differentiator

Competitive Edge: Distinctive Dominance is about carving out a unique position in the market that sets a business apart from its competitors.

Market Leadership: This force focuses on establishing a brand as a leader in its space, often through innovation, superior quality, or exceptional service.

The Synergy

Enhanced Value Proposition: Client Centricity ensures that the offerings are closely aligned with customer needs, while Distinctive Dominance ensures these offerings are not just tailored but also superior and unique in the market.

Sustained Loyalty and Growth: By combining Client Centricity with Distinctive Dominance, a business not only meets customer needs but also exceeds expectations, leading to increased loyalty, advocacy, and market share.

Feedback-Driven Innovation: Client Centricity provides valuable feedback and insights from customers, which can be used to fuel the innovation and differentiation strategies under Distinctive Dominance.

Brand Reputation: Distinctive Dominance helps in building a strong brand reputation, which is further enhanced by the positive customer experiences and relationships fostered through Client Centricity.

Conclusion

Client Centricity ensures that the business remains closely connected to the evolving needs and preferences of its customers, while Distinctive Dominance ensures that the business continues to stand out in a crowded market. Together, they create a powerful dynamic where customer-focused solutions are also market-leading innovations, driving both customer satisfaction and competitive superiority. This integration leads to a virtuous cycle of customer loyalty, market leadership, and sustained business growth.

Emotional Intelligence and Disruptive Mindset

Let's delve into how Emotional Intelligence and a Disruptive Mindset can be synergistically integrated:

EQ: The Human Connection

Understanding Emotions: EQ is about recognizing and understanding one's own emotions and those of others. It enables individuals to navigate social complexities with empathy and awareness.

Effective Communication: EQ is crucial for effective communication, conflict resolution, and building strong relationships, both within the team and with clients.

Disruptive Mindset: The Innovation Catalyst

Challenging the Status Quo: Disruptive Mindset involves questioning existing norms and processes, and being open to new ideas and approaches.

Risk-Taking and Adaptability: This mindset encourages taking calculated risks and being adaptable in the face of change, essential for innovation and progress.

The Synergy

Navigating Change with Empathy: Integrating EQ with a Disruptive Mindset means that while pushing for change and innovation, individuals also remain empathetic to the concerns and resistance that might arise from others.

Fostering a Supportive Environment for Innovation: Emotional intelligence helps create a supportive and understanding environment where team members feel valued and heard. This environment is conducive to the risk-taking and experimentation.

Enhanced Team Dynamics: An emotionally intelligent team can better handle the stresses and uncertainties that come with disruptive change.

Leadership and Influence: Leaders with high EI and a disruptive mindset can inspire and motivate their teams, drive change, and influence the broader organization to embrace new ideas and approaches.

Conclusion

This combination creates a powerful dynamic in an organization. EQ ensures that the pursuit of innovation and change is done with a deep understanding of and sensitivity to emotions, fostering a culture where change is embraced rather than feared. This integration leads to a more resilient, adaptable, and innovative organisation, where change is not only initiated but also effectively managed and embraced by all stakeholders.

Disruptive Mindset and Client Centricity

Integrating a Disruptive Mindset with client-centricity creates a unique and powerful approach to business strategy and customer relations.

Disruptive Mindset:
The Innovation Driver

Challenging Conventions: A Disruptive Mindset involves questioning and rethinking traditional ways of doing business. It's about seeking innovative solutions and being open to change.

Forward-Thinking: This mindset encourages looking ahead to anticipate market shifts and emerging customer needs, staying ahead of the curve.

Client Centricity:
The Customer Focus

Deep Understanding of Customer Needs: Client Centricity is rooted in a profound understanding of what customers truly need and value. It's about putting the customer at the heart of every decision.

Building Strong Relationships: This approach involves nurturing long-term relationships with customers, based on trust, reliability, and consistent value delivery.

The Synergy

Innovating with the Customer in Mind: By combining a Disruptive Mindset with Client Centricity, innovations are not just about being different; they're about being different in ways that matter to the customer. This alignment ensures that disruptive ideas are relevant and add real value to the customer.

Anticipating and Shaping Customer Needs: A disruptive approach, coupled with deep customer insights, can help in not just meeting existing customer needs but also in anticipating future needs and shaping them. This proactive stance can position a company as a market leader.

Enhanced Customer Experience: The fusion of these two forces can lead to the development of new products, services, or business models that significantly enhance the customer experience, leading to higher satisfaction and loyalty.

Feedback-Driven Innovation: Client Centricity ensures that customer feedback is integral to the innovation process. This feedback loop can inspire disruptive ideas and ensure they are grounded in actual customer needs and preferences.

Conclusion

The integration of these two creates a dynamic where innovation is not just about being different, but about being meaningfully different in the eyes of the customer. It ensures that the pursuit of novel and unconventional ideas is aligned with delivering real value. This approach not only drives business growth but also fosters stronger, loyal customer relationships, positioning the company as both innovative and customer-focused.

Disruptive Mindset with Distinctive Dominance

Combining a Disruptive Mindset with Distinctive Dominance creates a potent strategy for businesses, particularly in the competitive SaaS industry. Here's how these two forces can work together effectively:

Disruptive Mindset:
The Catalyst for Change

Innovation at the Core: A Disruptive Mindset is about embracing change and innovation, not just in products but in all aspects of the business.

Challenging the Status Quo: This mindset encourages questioning existing norms and practices, seeking out new opportunities and ways to stand out in the market.

Distinctive Dominance:
Establishing Market Leadership

Unique Value Proposition: Distinctive Dominance is about carving out a unique space in the market, where your product or service is not just different, but superior in addressing specific customer needs.

Sustained Competitive Advantage: This involves maintaining a position of strength in the market through continuous innovation and strategic positioning.

The Synergy

Driving Innovation with Purpose: The combination of a Disruptive Mindset with Distinctive Dominance ensures that innovation is not aimless. It's targeted towards strengthening the company's unique position in the market.

Creating and Capturing New Market Opportunities: A disruptive approach, when aligned with the goal of market dominance, can lead to identifying and capitalizing on new market opportunities before competitors do.

Reinventing and Reinvigorating Offerings: Regularly challenging the status quo keeps the product or service offerings fresh and ahead of the curve, reinforcing the company's dominant position.

Building a Brand of Innovation and Excellence: This integration positions the company as not just a market leader but as an innovator, enhancing brand perception and customer loyalty.

Conclusion

Merging a Disruptive Mindset with Distinctive Dominance leads to a powerful business strategy. It ensures that innovation is not just for the sake of being different but is directed towards strengthening and maintaining a unique and dominant position in the market. This approach not only helps in staying ahead of competitors but also in continuously delivering exceptional value to customers, thereby solidifying the company's market leadership and brand reputation.

Insight Agility with Customer Centricity

Integrating Insight Agility with Customer Centricity forms a dynamic approach that can significantly enhance a business's effectiveness, especially in sectors like SaaS where understanding and responding to customer needs is crucial.

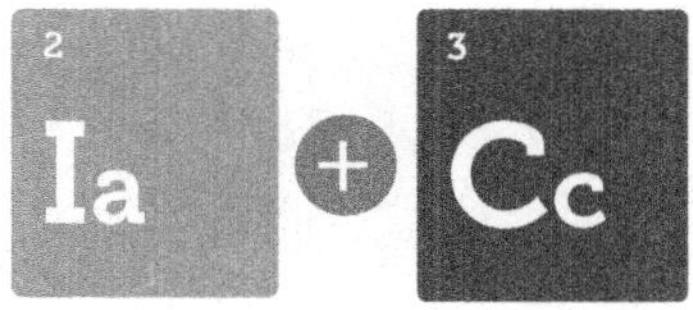

Insight Agility:
The Power of Understanding

Rapid Data Interpretation: Insight Agility focuses on quickly gathering and interpreting data to understand market trends, customer needs, and potential opportunities.

Adaptive Strategies: It enables businesses to adapt their strategies in real-time based on the insights gained, ensuring relevance and responsiveness.

Client Centricity:
The Heart of Business

Deep Customer Understanding: Customer Centricity revolves around deeply understanding and prioritizing customer needs, preferences, and pain points.

Tailored Solutions and Experiences: It involves creating solutions and experiences that are specifically designed to meet and exceed customer expectations.

The Synergy

Data-Driven Customer Understanding: Combining Insight Agility with Customer Centricity means that customer strategies are not based on assumptions but on real, actionable data.

Proactive Adaptation to Customer Needs: This integration allows businesses to proactively adapt to changing customer needs, ensuring that they are always offering relevant and valuable solutions.

Enhanced Customer Engagement: With rapid insights, companies can engage with customers more effectively, understanding their evolving needs and responding with tailored solutions.

Building Long-Term Relationships: The combination ensures that customer relationships are built on a foundation of understanding and adaptability, leading to stronger, more enduring connections.

Conclusion

The fusion of Insight Agility with Customer Centricity creates a business environment where understanding and responding to customer needs is not just a goal but a continuous process. This approach ensures that businesses are always aligned with their customers, leading to enhanced satisfaction, loyalty, and ultimately, business success. It's a strategy that combines the best of both worlds: the power of data and the importance of human connection.

Insight Agility with Distinctive Dominance

Merging Insight Agility with Distinctive Dominance creates a powerful combination that can propel a business to new heights, particularly in competitive markets.

Ia + Dd

Insight Agility:
The Backbone of Responsiveness

Rapid Market Analysis: Insight Agility involves quickly gathering and interpreting market data, customer feedback, and competitive intelligence.

Adaptive Business Strategies: It enables businesses to swiftly adjust their strategies based on the insights they gather, staying ahead of market trends and customer demands.

Distinctive Dominance:
The Mark of Leadership

Unique Value Proposition: Distinctive Dominance is about carving out a unique space in the market, offering something that sets the business apart from its competitors.

Market Leadership and Innovation: It involves not just competing but leading in the market through innovation and a strong brand presence.

The Synergy

Data-Driven Market Leadership: Combining Insight Agility with Distinctive Dominance means that the strategies for market dominance are continuously informed by fresh, relevant insights.

Proactive Market Positioning: This synergy allows businesses to proactively position themselves in the market, anticipating changes and adapting their unique value propositions accordingly.

Innovation Based on Real Needs: With a constant flow of market and customer insights, innovation becomes more targeted and effective, directly addressing emerging needs and gaps in the market.

Sustained Competitive Advantage: The combination ensures that the business not only achieves but sustains its competitive advantage by being agile and responsive to market dynamics.

Conclusion

The fusion of Insight Agility with Distinctive Dominance equips a business with the tools to not only understand the market in real-time but also to lead it. This approach ensures that a company's unique offerings are always aligned with market needs and are continuously evolving. It's a strategy that blends the agility to adapt with the vision to lead, ensuring long-term success and a strong, distinctive presence in the market.

Insight Agility with Emotional Intelligence

Combining Insight Agility with Emotional Intelligence creates a dynamic and empathetic approach to business, particularly beneficial in industries like SaaS where understanding both the market and the people within it is crucial. Here's how these two forces can synergize:

Insight Agility:
The Pulse of the Market

Rapid Data Interpretation: Insight Agility involves quickly gathering and interpreting data about market trends, customer behaviors, and industry shifts.

Adaptive Response to Market Changes: It enables businesses to swiftly adjust their strategies based on real-time insights, ensuring relevance and responsiveness.

Emotional Intelligence:
The Human Connection

Understanding Customer Emotions: Emotional Intelligence in a business context involves understanding and responding to the emotions of customers and team members.

Empathetic Communication and Relationship Building: It's about building strong relationships through empathetic engagement and effective interpersonal skills.

The Synergy

Empathetic Market Insights: Combining Insight Agility with Emotional Intelligence means that insights are not just data-driven but also empathetically informed, considering the emotional needs and responses of customers.

Responsive and Compassionate Business Strategies: This synergy allows businesses to develop strategies that are not only data-informed but also emotionally resonant with their target audience.

Building Trust through Understanding: By understanding the emotional landscape of their market, businesses can build deeper trust and loyalty with their customers.

Enhanced Team Dynamics: Emotional Intelligence also plays a crucial role internally, ensuring that teams are cohesive, communicative, and empathetically engaged, which is essential for agile responses to market changes.

Conclusion

The fusion of Insight Agility with Emotional Intelligence equips a business with a comprehensive understanding of both the logical and emotional aspects of its market. This approach ensures that a company's strategies are not only informed by the latest market data but are also empathetically aligned with the needs and emotions of their customers. It's a powerful combination that fosters deeper customer connections, trust, and loyalty, while maintaining the agility to adapt to ever-changing market conditions.

Client Centricity with Emotional Intelligence

Customer loyalty. Here's how these two forces can work together: Combining Client Centricity, and Emotional Intelligence forms an empathetic approach to business, and drives customer loyalty.

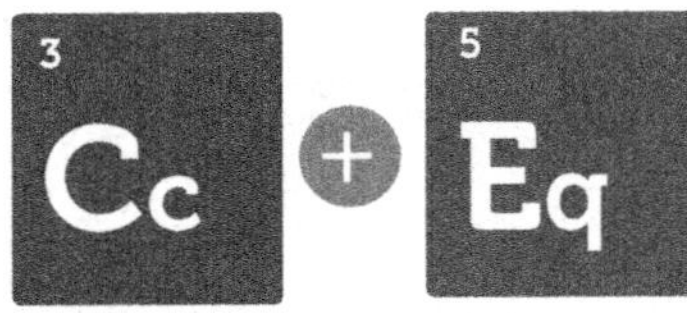

Client Centricity:
The Core of Business Strategy

Customer-Focused Approach: Client Centricity revolves around placing the customer at the heart of every business decision, ensuring that their needs and preferences drive the company's actions.

Tailored Solutions and Services: It involves creating products, services, and experiences that are specifically designed to meet the unique needs of each customer expectations.

Emotional Intelligence: Understanding and Responding to Emotions

Empathy and Emotional Awareness: Emotional Intelligence in a business context is about understanding and responding to the emotions of customers and team members.

Building Strong, Trust-Based Relationships: It's about using this understanding to build deeper, more meaningful relationships with customers.

The Synergy

Deep Empathy in Customer Interactions: Combining Client Centricity with Emotional Intelligence means that interactions with customers are not just about meeting their practical needs but also about understanding and responding to their emotional states.

Enhanced Customer Experience: This synergy allows for a more nuanced and empathetic customer experience, where customers feel genuinely understood and valued.

Proactive Problem Solving: Emotional Intelligence helps in anticipating customer needs and concerns, leading to proactive solutions that enhance customer satisfaction.

Long-Term Customer Loyalty: By consistently demonstrating empathy and understanding, businesses can foster a sense of loyalty and trust among their customers, leading to long-term relationships.

Conclusion

The fusion of Client Centricity with Emotional Intelligence is a powerful strategy for businesses looking to differentiate themselves in a crowded market. This approach ensures that customers are not only satisfied with the products or services offered but also feel emotionally connected and valued by the company. It's a holistic approach that considers both the practical and emotional aspects of customer service, leading to enhanced customer loyalty, satisfaction, and advocacy.

Distinctive Dominance with Emotional Intelligence

Combining Distinctive Dominance with Emotional Intelligence creates a powerful synergy that enhances a company's competitive edge while fostering positive, empathetic relationships with customers and stakeholders.

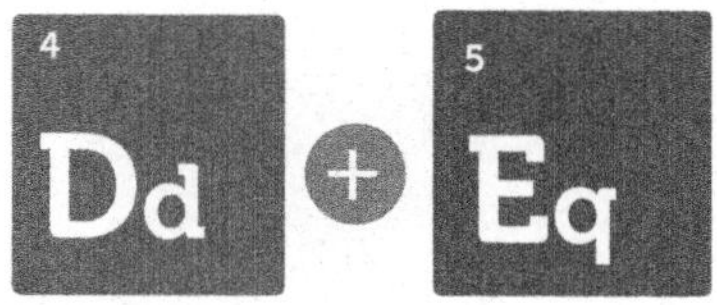

Distinctive Dominance:
Establishing a Competitive Edge

Distinctive Dominance: Establishing a Competitive Edge: Unique Value Proposition: Distinctive Dominance is about carving out a unique position in the market, offering something that competitors cannot.

Innovative Solutions and Practices: It involves innovating and continuously improving products, services, and customer experiences to stay ahead of the competition.

Emotional Intelligence:
The Human Connection

Understanding and Managing Emotions: Emotional Intelligence in a business context involves recognizing and appropriately responding to one's own emotions and those of others.

Empathetic Leadership and Communication: It's about using emotional awareness to guide decision-making, communication, and leadership.

The Synergy

Empathetic Market Positioning: Combining Distinctive Dominance with Emotional Intelligence means that market positioning and competitive strategies are informed not just by market data but also by a deep understanding of customer emotions and needs.

Customer-Centric Innovation: Emotional Intelligence allows for innovations and solutions that resonate on an emotional level with customers, enhancing their experience and satisfaction.

Building Trust and Loyalty: By understanding and addressing the emotional aspects of customer relationships, companies can build stronger, more loyal customer bases.

Adaptive and Responsive Leadership: Leaders with high Emotional Intelligence can better navigate market changes and challenges, ensuring that the company's distinctive dominance remains relevant and effective.

Conclusion

The fusion of both forces is a strategic approach that balances a strong competitive position with a deep understanding of human emotions. This combination ensures that a company's innovations and unique offerings are not only technically superior but also resonant with customers. It leads to a brand that is not only respected for its market leadership but also loved for its empathetic and human-centric approach. This synergy is particularly powerful in creating long-term customer relationships and a strong, enduring brand reputation.

The Power of a Triad

The integration of three distinct forces from our Five Forces model represents a powerful Triad that can significantly elevate a company's performance. This approach goes beyond the dual synergy of combining two forces, offering a more comprehensive, multi-dimensional strategy that addresses various aspects of business operations and market engagement.

The concept of blending three forces is akin to assembling a well-rounded team, each member bringing their unique skills and perspectives to the table. This triad approach allows for a more nuanced and robust strategy, as it balances innovation with empathy, data-driven insights with customer focus, and competitive edge with emotional awareness. For example, merging Disruptive Mindset with Insight Agility and Client Centricity can create a business environment that is not only innovative and data-savvy but also deeply attuned to customer needs and expectations.

The key advantage of this three-force combination is its holistic nature. It ensures that a business is not just excelling in one area but is capable of delivering exceptional performance across multiple domains. Whether it's driving innovation, understanding and meeting customer needs, or standing out in a crowded market, this triad approach provides a comprehensive toolkit for businesses to navigate complex challenges and seize opportunities.

In the following sections, we will delve into the dynamics of combining different sets of three forces, exploring how each combination can lead to distinct advantages and pathways to success. This exploration will demonstrate the transformative power of a multi-faceted strategy, highlighting how businesses can leverage these combinations to achieve a higher level of excellence and resilience in today's competitive landscape.

Disruptive Mindset, Insight Agility and Distinctive Dominance

Combining Disruptive Mindset, Insight Agility, and Distinctive Dominance creates a dynamic and powerful approach to business strategy and execution. This triad fosters innovation, responsiveness, and a strong competitive edge. Here's how these three forces can be integrated effectively:

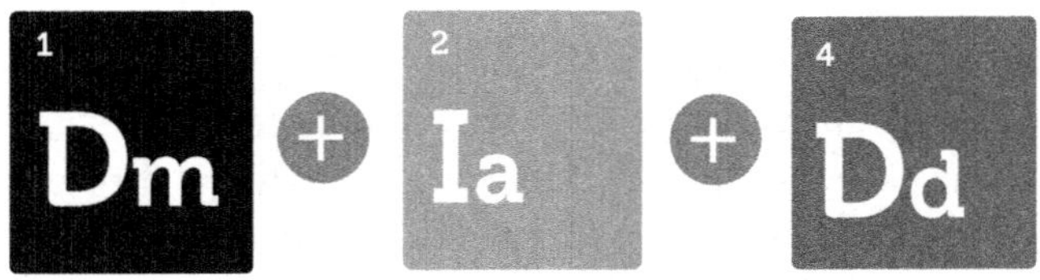

Disruptive Mindset:
Challenging the Status Quo

Innovation at the Core: A disruptive mindset encourages constant questioning of the norm and pushes for innovative solutions.

Risk-Taking and Experimentation: It involves being open to taking calculated risks and experimenting with new ideas. needs, staying ahead of the curve.

Insight Agility:
Leveraging Data-Driven Insights

Quick Adaptation to Market Changes: Insight agility ensures that the business can quickly adapt to changing market conditions and customer needs based on real-time data.

Informed Decision-Making: It involves using insights to make informed strategic decisions, enhancing the effectiveness of the disruptive mindset.

Distinctive Dominance:
Establishing Market Leadership

Unique Value Proposition: Distinctive Dominance focuses on creating a unique market position that sets the company apart from competitors.

Continuous Improvement and Innovation: It involves continuously refining products and services to maintain a competitive edge.

The Integration

Strategic Innovation: The combination of a disruptive mindset with insight agility leads to strategic innovation that is both groundbreaking and data-informed.

Responsive and Proactive Market Positioning: This triad allows a company to not only respond to market changes but also proactively shape market trends and customer expectations.

Balancing Risk with Informed Decisions: While the disruptive mindset encourages risk-taking, insight agility ensures that these risks are calculated and based on solid data. Distinctive Dominance then channels these efforts into a strong market position.

Sustainable Competitive Advantage: The integration of these three forces leads to a sustainable competitive advantage, as the company continuously innovates, adapts, and leads in its market.

Conclusion

The synergy of Disruptive Mindset, Insight Agility, and Distinctive Dominance creates a formidable approach to business strategy. This combination fosters a culture of continuous innovation, data-driven adaptability, and strong market leadership. It enables a company to not only anticipate and respond to market changes but also to actively drive and shape market dynamics. This integrated approach is key to building a resilient, forward-thinking, and dominant presence in any industry.

Client Centricity, Insight Agility and Emotional Intelligence

Combining Client Centricity, Insight Agility, and Emotional Intelligence forms a holistic and empathetic approach to business, particularly in customer relations and market responsiveness. This combination ensures that a company is not only data-driven and agile but also deeply attuned to the needs and emotions of its customers. Here's how these three forces can be synergizsed:

Client Centricity:
Focusing on Customer Needs

Deep Understanding of Customer Needs: Client Centricity involves a profound commitment to understanding and meeting the needs of customers.

Building Long-Term Relationships: It emphasizes nurturing long-term relationships based on trust and value.

Insight Agility:
Data-Driven Responsiveness

Real-Time Customer Insights: Insight Agility ensures that the company stays ahead of market trends and customer preferences through real-time data analysis.

Adapting Quickly to Customer Feedback: It allows for rapid adaptation to customer feedback, ensuring that products and services are always aligned with customer needs.

Emotional Intelligence:
Understanding and Responding to Emotions

Empathy in Customer Interactions: Emotional Intelligence brings a layer of empathy to customer interactions, allowing for a more nuanced understanding of customer needs and concerns.

Effective Communication: It enhances communication skills, ensuring that customer interactions are not only informative but also emotionally resonant.

The Integration

Empathetic and Data-Informed Customer Engagement: The combination of Client Centricity with Emotional Intelligence ensures that customer engagement is not only data-informed but also empathetically driven.

Responsive and Personalized Customer Experience: This trio enables the creation of a responsive and personalized customer experience, as insights are used to tailor interactions and responses to individual customer emotional states and needs.

Building Trust and Loyalty: By understanding and responding to both the explicit and implicit needs of customers, this integrated approach builds deeper trust and loyalty.

Enhanced Customer Satisfaction and Retention: The synergy of these forces leads to enhanced customer satisfaction and retention, as customers feel both understood and valued.

Conclusion

Integrating Client Centricity, Insight Agility, and Emotional Intelligence creates a powerful framework for customer engagement and satisfaction. This approach ensures that a company is not only responsive and adaptive to customer needs based on data but also deeply empathetic and emotionally intelligent in its interactions. It's a comprehensive strategy that leads to stronger customer relationships, enhanced loyalty, and a significant competitive advantage in understanding and meeting the evolving needs of the market.

The Quad Factor

The fusion of four forces creates a formidable synergy that can propel a company to new heights of success and innovation. This quadruple combination transcends the benefits of integrating two or three forces, offering a more layered and dynamic approach to business excellence.

Imagine this as a symphony where four distinct instruments come together, each contributing its unique sound to create a harmonious and powerful melody. In a similar vein, combining four forces in a business context allows for a multifaceted strategy that addresses a wide range of operational, market, and interpersonal dynamics. For instance, blending Disruptive Mindset, Insight Agility, Client Centricity, and Emotional Intelligence can lead to a business that is not only innovative and data-driven but also deeply empathetic and customer-focused, with a strong competitive edge.

The advantage of this four-force integration lies in its comprehensive coverage. It ensures that a business is well-equipped to handle various aspects of its operations, from fostering a culture of innovation and adaptability to deeply understanding and meeting customer needs, all while maintaining a competitive advantage and emotional intelligence. This approach is particularly effective in navigating the complexities and uncertainties of today's business environment, where agility, customer focus, and emotional acumen are as crucial as innovation and competitive positioning.

Let's explore the unique dynamics and benefits of different four-force combinations. This exploration will shed light on how businesses can strategically leverage these integrations to build a robust, resilient, and forward-thinking organization capable of thriving in the face of evolving challenges and opportunities.

Client Centricity, Distinctive Dominance, Disruptive Mindset, and Emotional Intelligence

Combining Client Centricity, Distinctive Dominance, Disruptive Mindset, and Emotional Intelligence creates a robust and multifaceted approach to business strategy and customer relations. This combination ensures that a company is innovative, empathetically engaged with its customers, competitively superior, and adaptable to market changes. Here's how these four forces can be synergised:

Client Centricity:
The Heart of Business Strategy

Deep Customer Understanding: Client Centricity ensures that every business decision is made with a deep understanding of customer needs and preferences.

Long-Term Customer Relationships: It emphasizes building and nurturing long-term relationships based on trust and mutual value.

Distinctive Dominance:
Establishing a Competitive Edge

Unique Market Positioning: Distinctive Dominance involves carving out a unique position in the market, differentiating the company from its competitors.

Leveraging Unique Strengths: It focuses on leveraging unique strengths and capabilities to create a competitive advantage.

Disruptive Mindset:
Innovation and Adaptability

Challenging the Status Quo: A Disruptive Mindset encourages challenging existing market norms and thinking innovatively.

Adaptability to Market Changes: It fosters adaptability and flexibility, allowing the company to pivot and innovate in response to market changes.

Emotional Intelligence:
Understanding and Managing Emotions

Empathy in Interactions: Emotional Intelligence brings empathy to all business interactions, ensuring a deeper understanding of both customers and team members.

Effective Communication and Relationship Management: It enhances communication and relationship management, crucial for internal team dynamics and external customer relations.

The Integration

Innovative and Empathetic Customer Engagement: Combining these forces ensures that customer engagement is innovative, empathetically driven, and strategically superior.

Responsive and Distinctive Customer Experience: This integration enables the creation of a distinctive and responsive customer experience, tailoring interactions to individual needs and emotional states.

Building Trust and Sustaining Competitive Advantage: By understanding and responding to customer needs innovatively and empathetically, this approach builds deeper trust and sustains a competitive advantage.

Enhanced Customer Satisfaction and Market Leadership: The synergy of these forces leads to enhanced customer satisfaction and positions the company as a leader in its market, capable of both anticipating and shaping customer desires and trends.

Conclusion

Integrating Client Centricity, Distinctive Dominance, Disruptive Mindset, and Emotional Intelligence creates a powerful and comprehensive business strategy. This approach ensures that a company is not only responsive and adaptive to customer needs but also innovative, empathetically engaged, and competitively superior. It's a holistic strategy that fosters strong customer relationships, enhanced loyalty, and a significant competitive edge in a dynamic market environment.

Distinctive Dominance, Insight Agility, Client Centricity, and Disruptive Mindset

Combining Distinctive Dominance, Insight Agility, Client Centricity, and Disruptive Mindset creates a dynamic and powerful approach to business strategy, customer engagement, and market positioning. This combination ensures that a company is not only ahead of its competition but also deeply attuned to its customers and continuously innovating. Here's how these four forces can be synergised:

Distinctive Dominance: Creating a Competitive Edge

Unique Market Positioning: Establishes a unique position in the market, setting the company apart from competitors.

Leveraging Strengths: Focuses on leveraging unique strengths and capabilities to maintain a competitive advantage.

Insight Agility: Data-Driven Decision Making

Responsive Market Strategies: Insight Agility ensures that decisions are data-driven, responsive, and timely.

Adapting to Customer Needs and Trends: It involves continuously adapting strategies based on evolving customer needs and market trends.

Client Centricity: Focused on Customer Needs

Deep Customer Understanding: Emphasizes understanding and meeting customer needs, preferences, and pain points.

Building Long-Term Relationships: Aims to build and nurture long-term, trust-based customer relationships.

Disruptive Mindset: Innovation and Flexibility

Challenging the Status Quo: Encourages innovative thinking and challenging existing market norms.

Adaptability to Change: Fosters adaptability and flexibility, allowing the company to pivot in response to market changes.

The Integratiom

Innovative and Customer-Focused Strategy: This combination ensures that the company's strategy is not only innovative but also deeply customer-focused.

Agile and Distinctive Market Positioning: Enables the company to quickly adapt to market changes while maintaining a distinctive position.

Data-Driven and Empathetic Customer Engagement: Integrating these forces allows for data-driven yet empathetic customer engagement, balancing analytical insights with a deep understanding of customer needs.

Sustaining Competitive Advantage through Innovation and Customer Centricity: By continuously innovating and focusing on customer needs, this approach sustains a competitive advantage and fosters long-term customer loyalty.

Conclusion

The synergy of Distinctive Dominance, Insight Agility, Client Centricity, and Disruptive Mindset creates a comprehensive and robust business strategy. This approach ensures that a company is not only competitive and innovative but also deeply attuned to its customers and agile in its responses to market changes. It's a holistic strategy that fosters strong customer relationships, enhanced loyalty, and a significant competitive edge in a dynamic market environment.

The Quintessential Fusion

In the realm of business strategy and organizational excellence, the integration of all five forces represents the pinnacle of strategic synergy. This quintessential fusion is akin to a master key, unlocking unparalleled potential and driving a business towards unprecedented success.

The Superpower of Combining All Five Forces

A Holistic Approach to Business Excellence

The combination of all five forces offers a holistic approach to business strategy. It ensures that every aspect of the business, from innovation and market insights to customer relationships and emotional acumen, is addressed and aligned. This comprehensive approach is crucial in today's complex business landscape, where a one-dimensional strategy is no longer sufficient.

Enhanced Adaptability and Resilience:

By integrating these diverse yet complementary forces, businesses can become more adaptable and resilient. Disruptive Mindset encourages constant innovation and adaptability. Insight Agility ensures that decisions are data-driven and timely. Client Centricity focuses on building strong customer relationships. Distinctive Dominance establishes a competitive edge, and Emotional Intelligence fosters a deeper understanding of both internal and external stakeholders. Together, these forces create an organization that can swiftly adapt to changes and overcome challenges.

Creating a Competitive Edge:

The fusion of all five forces provides a significant competitive advantage. It allows businesses to not only anticipate and respond to market changes but also to lead and shape industry trends. This proactive stance, supported by a deep understanding of the market and customers, sets a business apart from its competitors.

Building a Sustainable Future:

This integration is not just about immediate gains; it's about building a sustainable and prosperous future. By fostering a culture that values innovation, insights, customer focus, competitive strategy, and emotional intelligence, businesses are investing in a foundation that will support long-term growth and success.

The Power of Synergy:

The true power of combining all five forces lies in the synergy they create. This synergy amplifies the impact of each individual force, leading to outcomes that are greater than the sum of their parts. It's about creating an environment where innovation is fueled by insights, where customer relationships enhance competitive strategies, and where emotional intelligence informs every interaction and decision.

Combining all five forces creates a comprehensive and powerful framework for business success. This holistic approach ensures that a company is innovative, data-driven, customer-focused, competitively superior, and emotionally intelligent. Here's how these forces synergise:

4 Dd + 2 Ia + 3 Cc + 1 Dm + 5 Eq

Distinctive Dominance: Competitive Edge

Unique Market Positioning: Establishes a unique and superior position in the market.

Leveraging Unique Strengths: Utilizes the company's unique strengths to maintain a competitive advantage.

Insight Agility: Data-Driven Strategies

Responsive Decision-Making: Ensures decisions are informed by real-time data and insights.

Market and Customer Insights: Keeps the company attuned to market trends and customer needs.

Emotional Intelligence: Understanding and Empathy

Empathetic Leadership and Sales: Promotes understanding and empathy in interactions with customers and team members.

• **Effective Communication and Relationships:** Enhances communication skills and relationship-building capabilities.

Client Centricity: Deep Customer Engagement

Understanding Customer Needs: Focuses on deeply understanding and meeting customer needs.

Building Trust and Loyalty: Aims to build long-term relationships based on trust and value.

Disruptive Mindset: Innovation and Change

Innovation at the Core: Encourages constant innovation and challenging the status quo.

• **Adaptability:** Promotes adaptability to market changes and new opportunities.

The Integration

- **Innovative and Empathetic Business Culture:** Creates a culture that values innovation, customer focus, and emotional intelligence.
- **Data-Driven, Customer-Centric Strategies:** Combines datadriven insights with a deep understanding of customer needs for effective strategy formulation.
- **Adaptive and Competitive Market Positioning:** Ensures the company remains competitive and adaptable, with a strong emotional understanding of its stakeholders.
- **Holistic Approach to Business Challenges:** Provides a comprehensive approach to addressing business challenges, leveraging a blend of innovation, data, customer focus, competitive positioning, and emotional intelligence.
- **Sustained Growth and Customer Loyalty:** Fosters sustained growth, customer loyalty, and a strong competitive position in the market.

Conclusion

Integrating all five forces offers a robust and holistic strategy for businesses. This approach ensures that companies are not only ahead in terms of innovation and market positioning but also deeply connected with their customers and emotionally intelligent in their interactions. It's a comprehensive framework that fosters long-term growth, customer loyalty, and a significant competitive edge in a dynamic and challenging business environment.

Further Reading and Bibliography

Throughout the book we have discussed many topics and made references to different authors. Below are the references to those books and other articles and reading that you might find interesting on the different sections.

FORCE 1: Distinctive Dominance

Disruptive Mindset

1. Christensen, Clayton M. 1997. *The Innovator's Dilemma: When New Technologies Cause Great Firms to Fail.* Boston, MA: Harvard Business School Press.
2. Henman, Linda. 2021. *Risky Business: Why Leaders Must Develop a Disruptive Mindset.* Boca Raton, FL: Productivity Press.
3. Li, Charlene. 2019. *The Disruption Mindset: Why Some Organizations Transform While Others Fail.* Wharton School Press.
4. Ries, Eric. 2011. *The Lean Startup: How Today's Entrepreneurs Use Continuous Innovation to Create Radically Successful Businesses.* New York: Crown Business

Challenging the Status Quo

1. Ariely, Dan. 2008. *Predictably Irrational: The Hidden Forces That Shape Our Decisions.* New York: HarperCollins.
2. Bezani, Darren, and Jenni Bezani. 2023. *Unleash Your Sales Superpower: Emotionally Intelligent Selling.* London: Tricorn Books
3. Brown, Derren. 2006. *Tricks of the Mind.* London: Channel 4 Books
4. Cringely, Robert X. 1992. *Accidental Empires: How the Boys of Silicon Valley Make Their Millions, Battle Foreign Competition, and Still Can't Get a Date.* Reading, MA: Addison-Wesley Publishing Company.
5. Dixon, Matthew, and Brent Adamson. 2011. *The Challenger Sale: Taking Control of the Customer Conversation.* New York: Portfolio/Penguin.
6. Kahneman, Daniel, and Amos Tversky. 1979. "Prospect Theory: An Analysis of Decision under Risk." *Econometrica* 47, no. 2 (March): 263-291.
7. Kahneman, Daniel. 2011. *Thinking, Fast and Slow.* New York: Farrar, Straus and Giroux.
8. Grawitch, Matt. "Your Frame of Reference Influences Your Decision Making." Psychology Today. June 28, 2021.
9. Lakoff, George. 2004. *Don't Think of an Elephant: Know Your Values and Frame the Debate.* Vermont: Chelsea Green Publishing.
10. Sperry, Roger W. 1967. *Split-brain Approach to Learning Problems in The Neurosciences: A Study Program.* New York: Rockefeller University Press.
11. Zaltman, Gerald. 2016, *How Customers Think: Essential Insights Into the Mind of the Market.* Boston: Harvard Business School Press.

Continuous Evolution & Personal Vision

1. Collins, Jim. 1994. *Built to Last: Successful Habits of Visionary Companies.* New York: Harper Business.
2. Drucker, Peter F. 2006. *The Practice of Management.* New York: Harper & Brothers.
3. Halligan, Brian, and Dharmesh Shah. 2009. *Inbound Marketing: Get Found Using Google, Social Media, and Blogs.* New Jersey: Wiley

FORCE 2: Insight Agility

Building and Insight Factory

1. Aguilar, Francis J. 1967. *Scanning the Business Environment.* New York: Macmillan.
2. Argyris, Chris. 1977. *Double Loop Learning in Organizations.* Harvard Business Review 55 (5): 115-125.

Packaging Insight

1. Hopkins, Tom. 1980. How to Master the Art of Selling. New York: Warner Books.
2. Levitt, Theodore. 1983. The Marketing Imagination. New York: Free Press.

Sales Agility (Growth Mindset)

1. Dweck, Carol S. 2006. *Mindset: The New Psychology of Success.* New York: Random House.Konrath, Jill. 2014. Agile Selling: Get Up to Speed Quickly in Today's Ever-Changing Sales World. New York: Portfolio.
2. Landsberg, Max. 1996. The Tao of Coaching: Boost Your Effectiveness at Work by Inspiring and Developing Those Around You. London: Profile Books.
3. Ryan, Richard M., and Edward L. Deci. 2017. Self-Determination Theory: Basic Psychological Needs in Motivation, Development, and Wellness. New York: Guilford Press.
4. Vazzana, Michelle, and Lisa Sottosanti Doyle. 2023. The Sales Agility Code: Deploy Situational Fluency to Win More Sales. New York: McGraw-Hill.
5. Wiseman, Liz. 2010. Multipliers: How the Best Leaders Make Everyone Smarter. New York: HarperCollins.

FORCE 3: Client Centricity

Deep dive engagement

1. John Medina, 2014, Brain Rules: 12 Principles for Surviving and Thriving at Work, Home, and School. (Seattle: Pear Press)
2. Stephen Covey, 2013, *The 7 Habits of Highly Effective People: Powerful Lessons in Personal Change.* (New York: Free Press)
3. Sales Lion, 2023, *77% of B2B Buyers Do Their Own Research Before Speaking to Sales.* (Blog: Salesion.io)

Value Visualisation

1. Eric Loftus and Zanni, 1975. *Eyewitness testimony: The influence of the wording of a question.* (Bulletin of the Psychonomic Society, 5)
2. Neil Rackham, 1988, *SPIN Selling.* (New York: McGraw-Hill)
3. Mike Schultz and John Doerr, 2014, *Insight Selling: Surprising research on what sales winners do differently* (Hoboken, NJ: John Wiley & Sons, Inc.)
4. Gary Gaskell, 2018, *Value-Based Selling: How to Win Sales and Boost Profits by Understanding and Delivering Value.* (London, UK: Kogan Page)

Driving Lifetime Value

1. Jonah Berger, 2016, Contagious: How to Build Word of Mouth in the Digital Age. New York: Simon & Schuster
2. John Grinder & Richard Bander, 1975, The Structure of Magic: A Book About Language and Therapy (California, Science and Behaviour Books)
3. Sean Ellis & Morgan Brown, 2017, Hacking Growth. New York: Crown Publishing
4. Georgiana Laudi & Claire Suellentrop, 2023, *Forget the Funnel: A Customer-Led Approach for Driving Predictable, Recurring Revenue.* Lioncrest Publishing.
5. Julie Hogan and Nicholas Ezzo. 2019. *Customer Success: How Innovative Companies Are Reducing Churn and Growing Recurring Revenue.* Hoboken, NJ: Wiley.

FORCE 4: Disruptive Mindset

Competitive Advantage

1. Michael E Porter. 1985. Competitive Advantage: Creating and Sustaining Superior Performance. New York: Free Press.
2. Seth Godin. 2003. Purple Cow: Transform Your Business by Being Remarkable. New York: Portfolio.
3. Rita McGrath. 2013. The End of Competitive Advantage: How to Keep Your Strategy Moving as Fast as Your Business. Boston: Harvard Business Review Press.

Success Blueprint

1. Murphy, Lincoln, and Aaron Thompson. "Customer Success: How Innovative Companies Are Reducing Churn and Growing Recurring Revenue." San Francisco: Wiley, 2016.
2. Ries, Eric. "The Lean Startup: How Today's Entrepreneurs Use Continuous Innovation to Create Radically Successful Businesses." New York: Crown Business, 2011.
3. David Allen. 2001. Getting Things Done: The Art of Stress-Free Productivity. New York: Penguin Books.
4. Hyken, Shep. 2009 The Cult of the Customer: Create an Amazing Customer Experience That Turns Satisfied Customers into Customer Evangelists. Hoboken, NJ: Wiley.

Customer Advocacy

1. Arthur Carmazzi. 2017. Architects of Extraordinary Team Culture: 5 Secrets From the Ancient Pyramids. Kuala Lumpur: KV Publishing.
2. Frederick Reichheld. 1996. The Loyalty Effect: The Hidden Force Behind Growth, Profits, and Lasting Value. Boston: Harvard Business School Press.
3. V (VK) Kumar. 2012. Customer Lifetime Value: The Path to Profitability. Now Publishers Inc.
4. Kevin Roberts. 2004. Lovemarks: The Future Beyond Brands. New York: PowerHouse Books.

FORCE 5: Emotional Intelligence

Deep dive engagement

1. Wayne Payne, 1985, *A Study of Emotion: Developing Emotional Intelligence* (Cincinnati, OH: The Union Institute).
2. Willian Stern, 1914, *Intelligenzquotient*, 1912 original German edition by Stern, 1914 English translation by Whipple (Berlin: Zeitschrift für angewandte Psychologie).
3. Roger W Sperry, 1967, *'Split-brain Approach to Learning Problems.' In The Neurosciences: A Study Program* (New York: Rockefeller University Press).
4. Daniel Goleman, 2006, *Emotional Intelligence - Why it can matter more than IQ* (London: Bloomsbury Publishing)
5. Gerald Zaltman, 2016, *How Customers Think: Essential Insights Into the Mind of the Market* (Boston: Harvard Business School Press)

Motivation and Resilience

1. Pink, Daniel H. 2018. *Drive: The Surprising Truth About What Motivates Us*. New York: Riverhead Books.
2. Dweck, Carol S. 2006. *Mindset: The New Psychology of Success*. New York: Random House.
3. Covey, Stephen R. 2013. *The 7 Habits of Highly Effective People: Powerful Lessons in Personal Change*. New York: Free Press.
4. Benson, Herbert, and William Proctor. 2004. *The Breakout Principle: How to Activate the Natural Trigger That Maximizes Creativity, Athletic Performance, Productivity, and Personal Well-Being*. New York: Scribner.
5. Christensen, Clayton M. 1997. *The Innovator's Dilemma: When New Technologies Cause Great Firms to Fail*. Boston: Harvard Business School Press.
6. Loehr, Jim, and Tony Schwartz. 2003. *The Power of Full Engagement: Managing Energy, Not Time, Is the Key to High Performance and Personal Renewal*. New York: Free Press.

Empathy & Listening

6. Goleman, Daniel. 2006. Social Intelligence: The New Science of Human Relationships. New York: Bantam Books.
7. Marshall Rosenberg, 2015, Nonviolent Communication: A Language of Life. (Encinitas, CA: PuddleDancer Press)

8. John Medina, 2014, Brain Rules: 12 Principles for Surviving and Thriving at Work, Home, and School. (Seattle: Pear Press)

9. Paul MacLean, 2001, "The Triune Brain, Emotion, and Scientific Bias." In The Emergence of Neuroscience in the Twentieth Century, (edited by Stanley Finger, Franck Stahnisch, and François Boller, 219-232. New York: Springer, 2001).

10. Daniel Kahneman and Amos Tversky, 1979. Prospect theory: An analysis of decision under risk. (Econometrica, 47(2), 263-291)

11. Daniel Kahneman, 2013, Thinking, Fast and Slow. (New York: Farrar, Straus and Giroux)

Index

Printed in Great Britain
by Amazon

47537654R10159